Another
Weird Year

Another Weird Year

Huw Davies

cartoons by
Knife and Packer

EBURY
PRESS

1 3 5 7 9 10 8 6 4 2

Copyright © 2002 Huw Davies

Huw Davies has asserted his moral right to be identified
as the author of this work in accordance with the
Copyright, Designs and Patents Act 1988.

First published 2002 by Ebury Press,
An imprint of Random House,
20 Vauxhall Bridge Road, London SW1V 2SA
www.randomhouse.co.uk

Random House Australia (Pty) Limited
20 Alfred Street, Milsons Point, Sydney,
New South Wales 2061, Australia

Random House New Zealand Limited
18 Poland Road, Glenfield, Auckland 10, New Zealand

Random House South Africa (Pty) Limited
Endulini, 5a Jubilee Road, Parktown 2193, South Africa

The Random House Group Limited Reg. No. 954009

www.randomhouse.co.uk

Printed and bound in Great Britain by
Cox & Wyman Ltd, Reading, Berkshire

A CIP catalogue record for this book
is available from the British Library.

Cover designed by the Senate
Interior by seagulls

ISBN 0 09188 298 2

Contents

Introduction

Welcome to *Another Weird Year*. Over the last twelve months we've been treated to the full range of human idiocy, uncanny occurrences, natural wonders, animal antics and more. As you plunge into this catalogue of craziness it will, hopefully, give you what you are looking for: the occasional shudder of disgust, perhaps, at some of the more ghoulish events; disbelief at the depths of humankind's stupidity or at the freakishness of fate, closely allied with thankfulness that it hasn't happened to you – yet. Or maybe you just want a giggle.

Why do we still crave stories like these when it would appear that the world lurches from crisis to crisis? Wars still rage, terrorists attack, children perish in famines, floods and earthquakes wipe out thousands of people at a stroke. Yet, with all this, stories like those in *Another Weird Year* continue to take up newspaper column inches, fill magazine pages and feature regularly on news programmes.

The fact is that they offer comic relief from the 'real' news of economics and politics, disasters and murders that lead us to think that life is a very serious business indeed. They give us a chance to laugh at the world, yes, but they also remind us, no matter how obliquely, that life is a lottery. Nothing in life can be taken for granted, nothing is as certain as uncertainty and the only constant is change. And given that that is the case, it is distinctly less scary when viewed through the frame of exploding crows, cows dropping from the sky and elephants with road rage than through the grim and grisly events that make up the bulk of the actual news.

In the same vein, it is less disturbing to be reminded of the inescapable fact of human mortality (we *are* all going to die!) through an outlandish tale of a freak accident than to be faced with images of the body count from an air disaster or bomb attack that make us more and more scared to fly and increasingly wary of being around potential terrorist targets.

When it comes to human behaviour, we all know, deep down, that there's a wider range of activity than we may care to admit, and that the terms 'normal' and 'abnormal' may not even apply. (As film-maker Derek Jarman pointed out in reference to his outspoken approach to his own sexuality, 'Heterosexuality isn't *normal*, it's just *common*.') Read what some people do apparently without turning a hair or batting an eyelid and you'll come away confident and secure that whatever your own quirks, you're not abnormal. Uncommon, maybe – but that sounds far more agreeable than abnormal, doesn't it?

These stories have been sourced from all over the place. I've worked through mountains of newspapers and sliced them out with a scalpel (no nurse to mop my brow, unfortunately); I've perused magazines; I've searched the Internet, following leads here, there and everywhere; I've kept an eye on various newswires from press agencies; and I've had the help of a few story-clippers who have regularly sent me stories they have found.

Compiling the stories was enormously entertaining, but it wasn't all plain sailing, and before long I began to suffer from weird-fatigue. So many stories purporting to be weird passed before my eyes for evaluation and assessment. When I began collecting it was the opposite – I had a kind of weird euphoria. Every single story I had tracked down that had the weird or wacky label slapped casually on it seemed to be perfect, a magical distillation of all that was amazing and wonderful about humanity and the universe, bringing humour along with a fascinating slant on life that teaches us so much about ourselves. Robbers steal a cash box – which turns out to be empty! Hilarious and, of course, a classic morality tale. Man punches his lawyer in court. Gritty social commentary packaged in a truly slapstick moment (how hard do those kinds of professionals work for those who need them)?

Gradually, however, I came to see that most of those stories would never make the grade. My weird antennae tuned in. Man hit by flying cow. That's more like it. You couldn't make it up. Woman dials 999 to ask for sandwich. She must have done that with me in mind. Perfect. Baby's head moulded to make him look more like his father. Nasty, but wonderful. And so it went. But then, like a robust immune system subjected to too many boozy nights and dodgy takeaways, the strain began to tell. The reception on my weird antennae became a little fuzzy. My database of stories piled up, passing the thousand mark, but with every reading I found it more and more difficult to tell whether or not they were high-quality weird. Man steals underwear.

Terrific; or is it? Woman bumps into tree, false eye shoots out, lands in lap of man being loaded into ambulance to go to hospital (where they've just run out of false eyes) to have false eye put in; woman's false eye is found among folds of man's trousers and promptly used. Rubbish, happens every day, bin it. Or is it quite unusual after all?

Eventually I think I achieved a balance. In many of the stories it is the event itself or the final result that is funny or weird: live skunk found in box beneath sand, for example. And quite often the outcome of a weird event is unpleasant or sad, but in such cases it's the reason *why* the event happened that interests us more than its outcome. We don't like it when someone attempting suicide jumps off a bridge, but the fact that a queue of motorists urge her to do so because she is making them late for work tells us something about what people are capable of. It's not that we're making fun of others' misfortune – we're merely observing how humans, and the world, behave. And it does get pretty weird.

If you've been a regular visitor to the website, www.anotherweirdyear.com, you will already have been enjoying a daily selection of the year's weird, wild and wonderful stories. It is there that you can also add stories to the database (for inclusion in subsequent volumes), confirm the truth of others, or tell us when we've posted an urban myth masquerading as a real event (it invariably happens – and there may even be one or two lurking among these pages!). We'd love to hear from you, so visit the site and join in the fun.

Law&Order

NOT YOUR EVERYDAY CRIMES

Always know when to hold your tongue. Forty-nine-year-old Jeffrey Jacobitti, drove up to two women and a twelve-year-old girl and wiggled his tongue at them. He was arrested because, in the opinion of the deputy police chief of Keansburg, New Jersey, USA, wiggling his tongue constituted harassment that conveyed a threat. Especially when there was a child involved.

WEIRD

blow-up hold-up

An armed robber burst into an adult video shop in Winnipeg, Canada, brandishing a pepper spray, and screaming at the assistant and another man in the shop to put their hands up against the wall. The man demanded no cash but instead he grabbed what police referred to in their report as an 'anatomically correct sensation device' (we think that means a blow-up sex doll) worth over £180 and fled with it. Bob Johnson, spokesman for the Winnipeg police, said the robber was probably at home, enjoying himself. At that price, it must be quite a device.

In 2001 the city of Edmonton in Canada hosted the World Athletics Championships, and as part of the city's decorations twenty life-sized fibreglass bison were placed around the streets. It would appear that in one particular detail the bison were too realistic for someone who sliced the testicles from each and every model. Police were at a loss to explain the crime, while the chairman of the 'Buffalo Project' was in no doubt as to what should happen if the castrator was caught: 'Let the punishment fit the crime,' he said.

ASSAULT
...with edibles

As laughter swept through the courtroom, a fifty-year-old Toronto man was given twelve months probation on a charge of assault with a weapon – a lobster. The

...and wearables

A woman was arrested by Ontario Provincial Police having been accused of assaulting a policeman with her knickers. The arrest took place after the woman allegedly flagged down the police, demanding that they look for her shoes, then took off her pants and whipped an officer round the head with them. The unlucky (lucky?) policeman suffered no more than a red mark on his forehead, while the thirty-year-old woman from Sioux Lookout was charged with causing a disturbance.

victim suffered two small cuts to her hand when she deflected the crustacean and Mills was promptly arrested outside the store. Mills had become infuriated when the woman working behind the seafood counter requested that he did not put the lobsters on the scale himself. The clerk insisted on pressing charges of assault by lobster and Mills pleaded guilty as charged.

CRIMES INVOLVING BODILY FLUIDS

A Japanese teacher was arrested for wiping his saliva on a female passenger on a Tokyo commuter train. Forty-one-year-old Suburu Kimura put his fingers in his mouth then wiped spit down the woman's jacket. The woman claimed that this was not the first time that he had spat on her, although on this occasion her husband was on hand to grab the smutty saliva smearer and keep hold of him until the police came. It is not known what subject he taught, but it is doubtful that it had anything to do with hygiene.

Stephen Harris, thirty-nine, was charged with public indecency, but that was only because what he did was probably too disturbingly weird to qualify as a normal crime in the statute books. Harris was spotted on the surveillance camera at Lowes Home Improvement in Plainville, Connecticut, USA, unzipping his trousers and urinating just enough to slightly wet the back of the trouser leg of a man who was shopping at the store. He did it once without the

Police in Japan arrested a twenty-five-year-old woman who may have dumped more than a ton of vomit on the streets of the city of Anjo. Officers had been investigating forty complaints that puke had been mysteriously ditched around the city over a fourteen-month period, and had started staking out sites where they thought the culprit would strike again. Finally a woman was seen to drop three bags at a roadside and was arrested under local waste disposal laws. The bags were found to have a combined weight of over sixty-six pounds, giving rise to speculation that if she had been an active hurl-hauler for over a year the total dumped could have been more than a ton. The woman said that she was a bulimic and didn't want to dispose of her up-chuckings near her home.

man noticing, so Harris apparently returned and did it twice more. No motive was given in the police report, nor was there any evidence that the men knew each other.

An Ohio man was forced to wear a surgical mask in court while being tried for throwing saliva in Cincinnati, USA. Anthony Searles was convicted of one charge of inducing panic and two of criminal mischief and, to everyone's relief, was banned from working with food in prison. No fewer than thirteen women identified Searles as the man who targeted them as they were walking down the street. The forty-two-year-old's final downfall came when he spat into his hand and threw the saliva at an undercover female police officer.

STUPIDER THAN THE AVERAGE CRIMINAL

Any criminal who gets caught is stupid. Or at least not cunning enough to be a successful criminal. But here are some tales of miscreants who aren't even cunning enough to be called stupid. (Work that one out.)

Quit while you're ahead is a good philosophy, but not one heeded by the thief who went into a supermarket in Blackburn and stole three bottles of Jack Daniel's bourbon whiskey. He got away, but was arrested for shoplifting when came back for a bottle of Coke.

John Robert Broos Jr of Lino Lakes, Minnesota, USA, called the police to say he'd been beaten up and robbed. He even had the bumps and bruises to prove it ... except that he hadn't been robbed at all. He'd lost his money at a casino and, as surveillance cameras in a parking lot showed, he'd done the rough stuff to himself. He was seen to beat himself against a lamppost, rubbing dirt on to his face and even checking himself in his car mirror to make sure he looked just right. Broos was charged with obstruction.

Just how stupid do you have to be to boast about your crimes on stage in front of an audience? Glenn Matthews got up on stage with stand-up comedian Ricky Smiley (a stage name, surely) at the Comedy Café in Macon, Georgia, USA. To spice up the show Matthews launched into graphic descriptions of armed bank robberies, making his 300-strong audience chuckle and chortle. However, the club's owner, Mike Smith, a former policeman, was listening to the routine and decided that Glenn's art was imitating life a little too strongly for his liking. One phone call to the police later and Matthews was convicted of carrying out three local bank robberies. Not so funny.

Francisco Sanchez was arrested in Boston, USA on suspicion of drug dealing, and immediately

A man rammed a dog compound gate with his car to set free his pet husky, Rocky, who had been impounded after complaints from neighbours that he was a nuisance. Of course, the man, twenty-five-year-old Jamie Ferrucci of East Haven, Connecticut, USA, was charged with criminal trespass and criminal mischief. The really stupid thing was, as the assistant animal control officer pointed out, he need only have paid ten dollars to get his dog back. And, even more stupid, Rocky then ran away and wasn't found.

William Dykes was arrested after being identified on the security camera of a convenience store in Franklinton, Louisiana, USA, stealing cigars, cigarettes and alcohol. But when Dykes was confronted with the photographic evidence he tried to convince the police that the man caught on film rifling the shelves was in fact his evil twin brother, who follows him around wearing identical clothes and commits crimes using his identity. The police contacted Dykes's sister, to be told that he did have a brother – but that he wasn't his twin and he definitely wasn't evil. Police confirmed that they were confident they had the right man.

STUPID

tried to conceal his identity. The twenty-one-year-old bravely, if misguidedly, set about chewing off his fingerprints. And while he left his fingers a bloody mess and needed hospital treatment, his attempt failed.

 Enrique Aquilar Canchola, forty-two, tried, like many Mexicans, to make it across the border to the USA without being caught. His genius masterplan was to disguise himself as a seat! Enrique managed to hide himself inside the seat of a bus crossing the border at San Ysidro, California, but believe it or not, he was spotted and arrested by officials.

Nearly twenty years ago, Benjamin LaGuer was convicted of a brutal rape, and jailed in the MCI-

Steven McDonald, a forty-seven-year-old arson defendant decided to act as his own lawyer at his trial in Mount Vernon, Washington, USA. A key police witness had earlier testified that he saw McDonald at the scene of the fire 'arguing with himself'. When McDonald himself took the witness stand he posed questions as the lawyer, to 'Mr McDonald', the accused. McDonald (the lawyer) tried to get McDonald (the defendant) to say that the man seen arguing with himself could not have been him and must have been someone else: 'Mr McDonald,' he asked, 'have you ever talked to yourself?'

Norfolk prison, in Massachusetts, USA. For the whole of that time LaGuer manintained his innocence, and more recently asserted that DNA testing would prove it. His supporters mangaed to raise the 30,000 dollars needed for the test, and when the results came back … yes, it was LaGuer's sperm.

Meanwhile in Belleville, Illinois, USA, another alleged rapist was waiting for a DNA test that he was sure would prove his innocence. Marshall Thomas, forty-four, finally received the DNA test that would allow him to walk away from his 1999 rape charge. The test did indeed prove him innocent of the rape in question, however his DNA matched the profile from a different as yet unsolved rape and prosecutors planned to file charges.

BURGLARY PLUS

Burglars are supposed to get in, get the goods and get out, quick smart. But some housebreakers clearly want more spice in their lives than that and ensure that they enjoy their time inside someone else's property ...

A burglar broke into a house in Middlesbrough and helped himself to £8,000 worth of computer equipment. Feeling peckish and complacent, he then cooked himself a nice meal before getting away, leaving fingerprints on a cooking pot that helped police to track him down.

An intruder broke in to a house in Charmouth, Dorset stealing nothing at all, and leaving the owners better off to the tune of a television and a bottle of alcopop.

A sixteen-year-old Romanian burglar was caught red-handed – practising the piano. The young man said he broke in with the intention of burgling the house, but there was nothing of value there and since

ODD

Police in the Strausberg area of Germany are hunting a thief who breaks into people's bungalows, cooks himself a nice dinner, then washes up, leaving clean plates and an empty fridge. Police believe he may have struck up to 200 times.

he needed a spot of piano practice he thought he would get some in while he had the chance. Neighbours who knew no one was home were alerted when they heard music drifting from the house.

Think it's awful being held up and robbed? Not so for the employees of an Italian supermarket in Bassano del Grappa struck by a gang of seven rather civilised robbers. The gang members had coffee and chatted with the staff, apologising for having scared them, all the while ransacking the place for goods worth around £300,000. After an hour of polite pillage, they thanked the employees for their co-operation and slipped them £600 to share before making their getaway.

UNFEASIBLY LARGE THEFTS

Some thieves definitely think big.

Max Sneers went to harvest his field of lovely ripe corn near St Truiden, Belgium, but revved up his combine harvester in vain: someone had got there before him, leaving the field bare. The 2.5-hectare field which would have yielded 20 tonnes of corn for Mr Sneers, had been gathered by thieves in the night.

Thirty-two-year-old Gheorghe Lascarache spent the day away from his home in Roman City, Romania, jobhunting only to find on his return that it had been stolen. Not burgled – stolen. Thieves had demolished it and taken it, brick by brick. By the time police found one of the four culprits he had already sold his share of the loot for the equivalent of £2,000.

A sandalwood tree, believed to be the world's biggest, was stolen by no fewer than 100 armed robbers in the Indian state of Karnataka. The masked men attacked guards, sawed down the 18-metre, 150-year-old tree, loaded it on to a truck and escaped. Police blamed the 'sandalwood mafia'.

CRIME AND ARTIFICIAL LIMBS

A man tried to grab a handful of cash from the till of a hardware store in Kansas City, USA, and make a run for it but was tackled by a shop assistant as he did so. As he struggled to make off, his artificial leg came off (along with his trousers) in the assistant's hands, leaving the man to hop off at speed in his underwear towards a waiting getaway car.

Not quite a crime-and-artificial-limb story, but so nearly: Robert Bates, twenty-two, had agreed to act as lookout for friends during a burglary, in County Durham. The fact that he had drunk sixteen pints of

Dale Smith, forty-seven, was drinking at Incredible's Lounge, El Paso, Texas, USA, and had become so drunk that the waitress refused to serve him when he next ordered a drink. When he responded by burning her on the back of the neck with his cigarette, staff tried to eject him from the premises. Smith promptly pulled a gun and brandished it at the employees. However, in his drunken state he forgot that he had a false arm which promptly fell off, the hand still holding the gun. Gathering his arm and gun from the floor, Smith tried to leave, but by this time police had arrived and he was arrested at the door.

beer beforehand may go some way to explaining just why he took such a huge risk: Bates was literally (and figuratively!) legless. When the burglars were caught in the act by the homeowner, Robert tried to flee by shuffling on his bottom and pushing himself along with his hands. He was caught, inevitably, although, as the homeowner attested, he did move pretty quickly. If only he'd had an artificial limb or two …

Playing bowls with his team in Bradford, fifty-seven-year-old Ken Bedford was approached by a gang of young men. The lads refused to leave the bowling green, so eventually Ken threw cups of tea at them. A fight ensued between Bedford and one of the gang members, ending when the former's artificial leg fell off. Horrified, the young man and his mates fled.

NAKED CRIME

Picture this: a woman nicks your wallet and makes off down the street, discarding items of clothing as she runs. This is no male fantasy, but a real-life scam that has been going on in Hong Kong. Women pickpockets have been stripping off to avoid arrest, the idea being that they could accuse arresting officers of indecent assault. In the most recent incident a woman was accused of stealing a shopper's purse. When officers chased her through the streets of Kowloon she stripped right down to her knickers and escaped.

A gang of naked armed robbers raided a village in southern Bangladesh. Shocked villagers beat a hasty retreat, leaving the men free to enter the empty homes and rob them. When the bandits attacked the village of Nafitkhali Baattoli in the Sadar district of Bangladesh they made things even more difficult for the villagers by smearing their bodies with oil. The villagers knew that it would be impossible to overpower the men because they wouldn't be able to get hold of them. The police took a dim view of the whole situation and stated firmly that they shouldn't try it again because nude terrorism would be treated with a firm hand.

Illegal loggers on the Indonesian island of Sulawesi were apparently evading arrest by getting their wives to strip off, distracting government

Incensed by the number of advertising flyers enclosed in his local newspaper, the Moss Dagblad, in Norway, a man assaulted the woman who was delivering it. He covered her mouth and hit her on the head repeatedly, then escaped, naked, on a single roller skate. Eva Grading, the delivery woman, phoned the police on her mobile phone after scaring the man off with her screams. When the police finally caught up with and arrested the nude attacker he did not think he had done anything wrong. Well those flyers are annoying, aren't they?

BIZARRE

officials while they escaped with valuable hardwood. It seemed that the loggers knew that the authorities would be much too embarrassed to take action when faced with a bevy of naked women, no matter how tough they intended to be on the criminals themselves.

Apparently, in Miami, USA, it is a sin to praise the Lord in the nude. A man went to someone's front door on North River Drive to spread the good news about the Lord. A woman let him in, whereupon he preached (or 'ranted and raved about God', as she put it) and then stripped off, before running across the road and into another home. The owner there was far less charitable, and shot him. The naked man was expected to survive and the man who shot him was not charged, according to police.

ROBIN HOODS

Feared by the rich, loved by the poor ... and by other criminals as well.

Out on day leave from a Spanish prison in Aranjuez, near Madrid a fifty-four-year-old (inside for theft from a jewellery shop) succeeded in stealing £160,000 from a bank, after which he sent money orders (signed 'Robin Hood') to fellow inmates, then quietly returned to his cell. Following his return to prison, forty inmates received their money orders (totalling £5,000), but 'Robin Hood' did not manage to hide behind his new identity for long. On his next trip, the police (tipped off by prison authorities), followed him from Aranjuez to Madrid's main post office, and moved in as he started filling out money-order forms.

A bank worker stole from his bank to help hard-up customers and was jailed for his pains. Edward Hancock, father of two, was an account manager at an HSBC bank in Nottingham where he 'made available', as he would say, or 'stole', as the bank would say, over £17,000 for various customers in financial difficulties. He also increased overdraft limits without authority for some other customers and even took out a loan from a rival high-street bank in an attempt to cover his tracks. When the bigger overdrafts he set up were not repaid, he began stealing money from the accounts of Twycross Zoo Association, of which he was treasurer. Despite attempts to hide his Robin Hoodery, his crime came to light when the bank carried out a routine audit, and Hancock was jailed for fifteen months.

MUSIC SOOTHING THE FEVERED CRIMINAL BROW

On a crime-ridden street corner in West Palm Beach, Florida, USA, drug dealing, shootings and thefts all showed a decrease, thanks to the calming influence of Mozart, Bach and Beethoven. Police mounted a CD player and some speakers in an abandoned building and started playing a greatest hits-style compilation of the composers' music, loud enough to be heard clearly a block away. The number of loiterers has dropped too.

The British supermarket chain Tesco announced that trials of a new scheme to prevent motorists from driving away from their filling stations without paying for petrol proved successful and that the scheme will shortly be implemented. It involves playing the theme tunes from popular TV police dramas over loudspeakers, giving customers a subliminal reminder that the long arm of the law is never far away.

GIVING THEM MORE THAN THEY BARGAINED FOR

A Lancashire woman fought off three armed robbers by squirting them in the eyes with washing-up liquid. Julie Walsh was cleaning when a gang of robbers, armed with pistols and wearing balaclavas burst into her shop in Helmshore, Lancashire. Showing great

A masked armed robber beat a retreat after walking into a bakery in Frankenthal, Germany. When he pointed his gun at the woman behind the counter and demanded money, she not only refused but started to bombard him with a volley of bread rolls and sticky buns, at which point he turned and ran.

presence of mind and even better aim, Mrs Walsh squirted the robbers in the eyes with her washing-up liquid, shouting, 'Get out'. Which they did, empty-handed.

Jacqueline Duncan, of Philadelphia, USA, answered a knock at her door to find a man dressed in a postman's uniform. When he asked her to open the door to sign for a package, she smelt a rat

BEWARE OF THE CAT

and refused. The man then pushed his way into the house and a struggle ensued. Suddenly, Jacqueline's three-year-old tabby cat, Whiskers, also smelling a rat, burst into hall, leapt up at the intruder and bit him. The man turned and ran, leaving behind some strapping with which he was attempting to tie up his victim.

A robber in Caversham, New Zealand, certainly got a good deal more than he bargained for when he tried to rob the Mayflower takeaway. The masked man threatened the owner, Jim Tran, with a knife, at which Tran promptly pulled out a meat cleaver. The would-be robber, sensing that he was now at something of a disadvantage, ran away.

In the French port of Calais, an armed robber struck in the car park of a hypermarket where three English women were on a shopping trip. The robber got into their car, pointed his gun at them and tried to drive off. But that's when things got a bit difficult. Jean Douglas, the seventy-one-year-old driver, began hitting him, while Ann Aylward, sixty-nine, and sitting in the back seat, grabbed him around the neck. Joan Windsor, seventy, who was outside the car, then reached in, grabbed the gun and began to pound the robber on the head with the butt. When the robber still managed to get the car moving, Aylward tightened her grip on his throat, choking him and yanked his head over to one side so that he crashed the car. At this point he gave up and ran off, battered and bruised.

SMUGGLING STUFF INTO PRISON

Well how else are you supposed to get hold of the things you need when you're inside?

An eighty-four-year-old Greek woman was bringing her jailed grandson a lovely spaghetti and meat sauce dinner (just like grandma used to make), when prison officials noticed she was acting suspiciously. Inside the bowl, which had a double bottom, they discovered a 30-gram packet of heroin.

They couldn't very well have been smuggled in inside a cake – prison officials found two twenty-litre beer barrels hidden in a solitary confinement cell in the Vila Branca prison in Sao Paulo, Brazil. The police

Speaking of getting a fix in jail, a Canadian newspaper was investigating the death of an inmate in the Pine Grove Correctional Centre in Saskatchewan and discovered that a rather desperate way of getting high was the cause of the death. It was reported by witnesses inside the centre that some formerly heroin-addicted female inmates so desperately craved methadone that they routinely consumed the fresh vomit of inmates on methadone treatment for traces present in the regurgitation. The dead inmate had, in fact, choked on someone else's vomit.

STRANGE

chief is sure that it was an inside job, since the barrels did indeed arrive during visiting hours.

Police in Peru arrested a gang trying to smuggle 200 chickens stuffed with cocaine into a prison. They were seized as they tried to enter Lima's San Pedro prison. The plucked chickens were found to contain a total of ten kilos of cocaine. Police thought the gang was working in partnership with a guard at the prison.

GETTING OUT OF JAIL

The world record for being on the run was broken by jailbreaker John Hannan. Police were half hoping he would give himself up just for the sake of getting his name into the *Guinness Book of Records*, but weren't holding their breath. Hannan had avoided recapture for an amazing forty-six years, just beating the forty-five years and eleven months of American Leonard Frisco who was turned in by his son after an argument. Hannan was sentenced to twenty-one months in Verne Prison in Dorset, having been convicted of car theft and assaulting police officers in 1955, and escaped after just thirty-one days.

A prisoner walked out of Los Angeles County Central Jail by pretending to be a prison official. The key to his escape was a fake ID card he had made using a picture of film star Eddie Murphy taken from a magazine advertisement for Dr Dolittle 2. Convicted earlier for attempted murder, Kevin Pullum was still wearing the civilian clothes in which he had made his court appearance, so it's safe to assume that security at the jail may just have to be tightened up a little following this incident.

There was a spectacularly unsuccessful escape attempt from the Bangu prison in Rio de Janeiro, Brazil, when an unnamed inmate dug a tunnel to escape and his sense of direction went seriously awry. The tunnel led into the cell of another prisoner and on the day our hero made his bid for freedom he popped up in the said cell, right in front of some prison warders. He swiftly turned round and rejoined the rest of the gang in the exercise yard. Meanwhile, the warders claimed that they hadn't seen enough of him to be able to positively identify him, so he went unpunished both for his escape attempt and for his stupidity.

A prisoner at a top-security jail on the Isle of Sheppey, Kent, very nearly made a highly ingenious escape using the combined powers of brown sauce and electricity. Making a chain out of his foil food trays, Nicholas Kelleher connected them to the electricity socket and added the brown sauce, whereupon the reaction between the electricity and the acid in the sauce burned the metal bars of his cell. The fatal flaw in the plan was, as usual, pride. Kelleher boasted to a fellow inmate that he had burned through one of the bars, with only two more between him and escape. The inmate, of course, blew the whistle on him.

An inmate at Okanogan County Jail used dental floss and toothpaste to saw his way through a fence and escape. When Scott Brimble complained of claustrophobia he was left in the exercise yard of the jail in Washington State, USA, where he got on with the job of using his dental hygiene products to weaken the wire mesh in the fence before making his getaway.

BREAKING INTO JAIL

A prisoner escaped from his jail in Chile to meet up with a few mates in a local bar and have a booze-up. When the session was over, Cecilio Emilio Ritz, accused of murder, lurched back to Yungay Prison and demanded to be let back in. He waved at the guards and tottered back to his cell where he fell asleep. The bemused guards had already started a search for Ritz, who later said that he had decided to risk being shot escaping rather than miss knocking back some beers with his friends. Ritz was later transferred.

Some of those low-security prisons are just too cushy to give up. Trouble is, they don't supply enough beer and ciggies. Mark Delude, thirty-nine, was reported missing from the St Johnsbury work camp in Vermont, USA, where he was serving a sentence for a variety of minor offences. Delude escaped from the low-security jail by crawling under the fence. He then walked the mile and a half to the nearest convenience store, bought a twenty-four-pack of Budweiser, a carton of cigarettes and a lighter before making his way 'home'. Back at the jail, he found a welcoming committee of guards who had not been remotely fooled by the bunched-up clothing he'd left under his sheets as a foil. Delude admitted that he had been drinking home brew before nipping out on a beer run. After he was caught he was returned to custody and transferred to a prison with a secure perimeter fence system. And that beer run could get him two more years behind bars.

 Two men broke into a prison in Arad, Romania, to steal 40 kilos of cabbages from the kitchen. They jumped over the fence, beat up a guard who disturbed them, and grabbed the vegetables. The guard managed to call for help and the thieves were eventually caught – and now face a sentence in the very jail they robbed. At least they won't have to eat cabbage soup when they get there.

GETTING IT IN JAIL

Prison guards at the jail in Osorno, Chile, held fundraising events to pay for prisoners' conjugal visits. The convicts had complained that being deprived of sex was an extra, and unfair, punishment on top of their prison sentence, and the warders agreed. So they sold raffle tickets and held a bingo night inside the prison, and the cash raised was used to provide a 'matrimonial suite' and to pay for the travel costs of female visitors.

Two Indonesian prison guards helped an inmate to escape to a brothel for the night because they thought he deserved a break. Plain-clothes police officers re-arrested the prisoner after bumping into him during a routine drugs operation. Police said that one of the guards told officers he had helped the inmate to escape for 'humanitarian reasons'.

BEING LESS THAN RESPECTFUL IN COURT

A thirty-nine-year-old woman got the result she wanted when she was found not guilty of abducting her children in a divorce fight in Toronto, Canada. Just a few short minutes later, however, she was convicted of contempt of court because she just wouldn't stop putting her finger in her mouth and making popping sounds while the judge was speaking.

A UK man in court on charges of disorderly behaviour and criminal damage to a police van could not be persuaded to take off the pink plastic pig's nose he wore for his court appearance. Despite being sent to the cells to change his mind, forty-seven-year-old Gordon Palmer ignored all demands to remove the offending snout and was consequently jailed for fourteen days. (His gesture had, of course, been a protest against police treatment.)

LAWSUITS

Suing when something goes wrong seems to be a knee-jerk reaction in some places (the emphasis being on 'jerk').

Kane Rundle, twenty-two, filed a lawsuit for 1 million Australian dollars against the New South Wales State Rail company, after he suffered severe injuries from an incident in which, when leaning out of the window of a moving train and spraying graffiti, he hit his head. The argument put forward by Kane's lawyers was that since the rail company were aware that certain passengers sprayed graffiti out of windows they should have been doing more to prevent it.

 The parents of University of Florida student Matthew Kaminer filed a lawsuit against the Eckerd drugstore chain and the manufacturer of the powerful painkiller OxyContin when their son died following an overdose on the drug after a friend of his had stolen it from an Eckerd drugstore. The parents claimed that Eckerd should have protected its supply of OxyContin better so that their son would not have been tempted to take it.

 A man who strapped pork chops to his feet and walked through a hotel was sued by another customer who said he slipped on the fat from the chops. Ross Lucock won the chops in a meat raffle during a night out at the Jannali Inn, Sydney, Australia. Troy Bowron says he was playing pool in the hotel when he slipped on the pork fat and broke two bones in his left arm.

 The Barnet Motor Inn in Vancouver, Canada, boasts exotic dancers; but what they don't tell

POLE
DANCE = $20

LAP
DANCE = $50

KICK
IN THE = P.O.A.
HEAD

you is just how close to them it's safe to sit. That was Greg Bonnet's problem, and he sued them after his nose was broken by a kick from a stripper as she swung round a pole. The stripper was also sued for dancing in a reckless and negligent manner.

A Toronto woman took her lover to court because – from her point of view – he was cheating on her with his wife. Eunwoo Lee claimed £102,000 from John Riley on the grounds that for the four years they were seeing each other he never mentioned that he had a wife, and she, as a result had been taken out of the singles market.

medication maniac

A fifty-three-year-old businessman from north London was chasing £8.5 million in compensation from a pharmaceutical company for the side-effects of a drug he had taken for a non-malignant tumour. Doctors had warned Richard Davis that the drug, Bromocriptine, might cause a blocked nose. But Mr Davis claimed that the medication had transformed him from a quiet, bridge-playing virgin to a cross between a deranged sex maniac and a highly over-excited teenager who frequented karaoke bars. He started buying pornographic videos and became promiscuous, paying for sex with call girls on week-days and enjoying 'extremely active' weekends with his girlfriend. Since the case, demand for Bromocriptine in Britain has skyrocketed.

The University of South Florida found itself in a little legal trouble when a lawsuit was filed against it for religious discrimination by two ex-members of the medical faculty. It turns out that the former chairman of the medical school, a Dr James Rowsey, had denied researchers vital equipment on the authority of his wife. Being henpecked is not unusual (we all know that Ronald Reagan took lots of decisions on Nancy's say-so) but even Ronnie didn't believe his wife was a prophet, as Dr Rowsey did. Dr Rowsey had also pressured faculty members into praying that the university administration would increase the department's budget.

Howard Strumph filed a lawsuit against the police department of Voorhes, Pennsylvania, USA, claiming that they were responsible for his wife's death in 1999. The police had failed to enter the house and save Mrs Strumph when she was shot by someone whom they believed to be a homicidal maniac. That someone, however, was Mr Strumph himself, who had just shot his wife, along with the handyman employed by the couple. In fact, Strumph had been aiming for the handyman who was attacking his wife, but being wheelchair-bound, his aim was a little shaky and he shot his wife in error.

This is a suit that the plaintiffs won and it's not hard to see why, really (although we might struggle to see how the plaintiffs believed what they were told). Kaziah Hancock and Cindy Stewart won almost $300,000 in damages when they sued self-proclaimed prophet Jim Harmston, of a breakaway Mormon sect. The two claimed that they were the victims of fraud, Harmston having failed to deliver on several promises he had made to them in return for money (one such promise being that he would produce Jesus Christ himself, in the flesh). Hancock also gave 67 acres of land to the church in return for a house, but after the church had made one payment on the house, payments were halted when Harmston claimed that God had told him to stop paying.

It's nice when your students are quick learners. Not so nice though when it backfires on you, as University of Virginia tort professor Kenneth Abraham learned. As part of his lecture on 'assault and battery' Abraham explained how even the slightest unwanted physical contact can be costly if the 'victim' is vulnerable in any way. By way of demonstration he then went on to tap the shoulder of a random student. The student in question, however, was Marta Sanchez, who unbeknown to Abraham had recently been raped. Consequently, the tap on the shoulder triggered 'fear and distress', and Sanchez filed a $35,000 lawsuit

chimps in court?

A new group has sprung up in the USA. It's called the Chimpanzee Collaboratory, and it's a coalition of researchers and animal welfare advocates who contend that the 1,500 chimpanzees curerntly held in captivity in the USA need legal protection from abuse by humans. In effect, they are planning to enable chimpanzees to sue in a court of law, represented by third parties such as animal rights activists. They base their arguments on the fact that chimpanzees are roughly as intelligent as a three-year-old child, and that if children enjoy legal status through their guardian, then so should chimps. It may be some time before we hear of a law suit being taken up by a chimp against its exploitative owners, but the wheels have been set in motion...

ODD

let's forget about it

Down in the Deep South of the USA they do things differently, especially when it comes to interaction between the sexes, it would appear. According to a lawsuit launched last year, the manager of a Wal-Mart in South Carolina was informed that one of his employees had fondled a ten-year-old girl in the store. The good-hearted manager's response was to offer the little girl's mother a twenty-five dollar Wal-Mart gift certificate to forget about the whole thing.

against Abraham, claiming that the tap indeed constituted assault and battery.

THE PETTY ARM OF THE LAW

Sometimes law enforcers really need to lighten up, chill, take it easy, not come down too hard … but sometimes they just can't bring themselves to do that. The law is the law, after all.

The US state of Texas is known for its hard line on crime, so it's not too surprising that Sweetwater Library has been issuing warrants for the arrest of people keeping overdue books. Technically, this is, after all, theft of public property, carrying a maximum penalty of six months in the slammer and a $2,000 fine.

Eighty-five-year-old Erich Butler of Potsdam, Germany, was fined the equivalent of £67 after the town's official grass checkers noticed that the grass on his lawn was more than a foot high. Erich Butler had been too ill to trim his lawn, and while a spokeswoman for the town council said they might not have fined him had they known he was ill, a refund of the fine would now be out of the question, as it would be against the law ...

... And the vegetation height fascists were out in force in California too, making sure shrubs stayed short and sweet. Software engineer Kay Leibrand was the first person to face criminal charges having been arrested and fingerprinted under a public-nuisance law in Palo Alto prohibiting any shrub more than 2 feet high on the strip of land between the road and the pavement. The sixty-one-year-old said she wanted to be screened from the traffic, so she let her shrubs grow up to 6 feet in places. As a result she faced a maximum fine of $1,000 and up to six months in the county jail for her shrub-based criminality.

A Belgian baker did his best to help his local festival by baking a gigantic cake for charity. But the fruit and cream cake, big enough to feed 1,500 people, was banned by Belgian food inspectors and could not be eaten because it broke regulations. The food inspectors (tipped off by a rival baker) ruled that the cake could not be sold unless it was kept at a constant 7°C, and since it was too big to go into a refrigerator it had to be thrown away.

BIZARRE

dobbin parked

Robert McFarland, a former blacksmith in Skipton, a market town in the Yorkshire Dales, who uses his horse Charlie Boy for horse and cart tours of the town, was staggered to find his horse had been given a parking ticket. Under the heading 'vehicle description' the overzealous, highly conscientious but not very imaginative traffic warden had put 'brown horse'.

A South African motorist who was stopped by traffic police on his way to work in Pretoria had his car confiscated and was fined, for the chillingly callous crime of giving three friends a lift to work. John Motsoa, according to the arresting officers, was operating an illegal taxi service because none of his friends, who were contributing to petrol costs, owned a car. (Curiously, if they had owned cars, even though they weren't using them, it would have been fine.) To add insult to injury, while Mr Motsoa was waiting for his car to be returned he had to travel to work by taxi.

An Italian motorist left his car briefly to go into the traffic warden office in his home town of Trento and pay the fines from previous parking tickets. On returning to his car Diego De Carli discovered that he had been given another parking ticket. He went back inside to protest, was promptly rebuffed, then came out again to find a second parking ticket placed on top of

game playing

The residents of Ashton, Cornwall, fought a long and drawn-out twenty-five-year battle with their local council to have a playing field laid out in their village. When the council finally gave in and the residents finally got their playing field, the council informed them that it could not actually be used for organised sports.

the first. Back again he went only to be met with riotous laughter and the consolation that he might not have to pay for the second ticket.

An Arizona couple was arrested for the foul and heinous crime of leaving their Christmas lights up for too long. Law officials said that Angelica and Tony Flores were in transgression of a code requiring decorations to be removed nineteen days after the holidays, and went on to point out that the offending decorations were still on show in April. Still up in April? Some people...

A taxi driver was told that his black cab wasn't black enough and that he would not be allowed a cab licence to work in the city of Newcastle. Although the log book of Khalid Hussain's Vauxhall Vectra describes it as black, the council official sent to inspect it for blackness detected a hint of grey and proclaimed it not black enough.

A town council in South Wales banned a two-year-old boy from playing with his plastic golf set in his local park. Rules state that golf must not be played, so aspiring golfer Daniel Williams, whose longest drive with his plastic club and ball is 7 feet has been forced to play elsewhere.

An Australian man who broke wind in the foyer of a Melbourne police station had his conviction for offensive behaviour overturned after the prosecution failed to prove that flatulence was a voluntary act. David Grixti had already been fined $A200 after being arrested for drinking offences, and it was in the police station that he fell foul of the fart police.

Gender-equality ombudsman, Ms Ausrine Burneikiene of Lithuania, announced that she would fight to end a law necessitating gynaecological

STRANGE

power game

Italian police forced a driver to search for three hours for a cigarette end he had flicked out of his window. The officers saw the butt land on the side of the motorway at the Brennero pass and pulled the motorist over, watching while he searched a half-mile stretch for three hours without success. Eventually they gave him the mandatory fine of 19 euro (for breaking the Italian law forbidding the throwing of things out of a car window) and let him go.

examinations for women before they are granted a driving licence. The rather strange requirement is based on the belief that some female illnesses manifest themselves suddenly or cause unconsciousness and are, as such, a danger to other motorists.

A Dutch couple, Jan and Juliana Sijtsma, who were celebrating their wedding day, hired a stunning vintage car, a 1917 Buick, to carry them from the wedding ceremony to the reception, in the town of Leeuwarden. But wouldn't you just know it, Officer

smoking out the smokers

Is this the ultimate in pettiness and an infringement of civil liberties, or a sophisticated appreciation of what good health care should be? Decide for yourself ...

The Montgomery County Council near Washington DC, has introduced a law that means people will have to stop smoking in their own homes if it annoys their neighbours. That means that if smoke drifts into someone's house, through a door, or a vent, or an open window, the neighbour will be entitled to complain. Smokers could face fines of up to $750 if they fail to address the problem after a complaint has been made. Council member Isaiah Leggett was at pains to point out: 'This does not say that you cannot smoke in your house. What it does say is that your smoke cannot cross property lines.'

PECULIAR

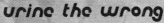

urine the wrong

On seeing a man urinating in public, the mayor of Calcutta, Subrata Mukherjee, resorted to instant justice and thrashed the offender's backside with a branch. Mukherjee said that because existing laws were not strict enough, and proving that someone had urinated in public was a long procedure (and the fine was ridiculously low anyway), an on-the-spot penalty was the best course of action. He won wide support from colleagues and members of the public.

Jobsworth out on his police motorcycle, spotted what he thought was an illegal car and pulled them over, fining them for driving an unroadworthy car. Later, an Automobile Inspection spokesman confirmed that the car had been checked and approved as roadworthy.

CRIME AND PUNISHMENT

As prisons become more and more overcrowded, law enforcers are forced to be more creative with their sentencing ...

When Leslie Thompson, forty-eight, of Hot Springs, Arkansas, USA, was convicted of her second shoplifting offence in a year, the judge gave her a choice: three days in jail or standing outside the DIY

justice?

After pleading guilty to stabbing a man, Leah Marie Fairbanks, twenty-five, of Duluth, Minnesota, USA, was sentenced to fourteen months' probation. The sentencing judge declared that she was to read the Declaration of Independence, as well as seven classic novels, and to write reports on each. This would give her time to reflect upon the nature of her crime, allowing her to grow as a person. Her co-defendant, meanwhile, was sentenced by a different judge: she got eight years in prison.

shop where she was caught, with a sign reading, 'I am a convicted shoplifter'. Thompson opted for punishment by humiliation rather than incarceration.

For those who hate it when someone drives past with their windows down and their car stereo loud enough to rattle your window-frames – this story is for you (except the punishment might not seem severe enough):

Alan Law, of Cleveland, Ohio, USA, was found guilty of disorderly conduct for driving through town with his music way too loud, and was given a choice by Judge John Nicholson between listening to polka music as performed by Cleveland polka legend the late Frankie Yankovic, or paying a fine. Law chose polka and spent four hours sitting in a police interview room listening to hits like 'Blue Skirt Waltz', 'Who Stole the Kishka' and 'Too Fat Polka'. Judge Nicholson hoped that Law would learn just what it feels like for people to have to listen to music they don't like.

There are no kangaroos in Poland, but as for kangaroo courts ... A shoplifter in the city of Szczecin received instant justice when supermarket staff found him trying to steal a shirt. One swift call to 'The Boys', and minutes later a Mercedes with blacked-out windows rolled up and a group of men got out to deal with the offender. They stripped the nineteen-year-old naked and wrote 'I am a thief' on his back before leaving him in the city centre.

Animals

BEING SLAIN

At a school for disabled children in the Japanese city of Tottori eleven rabbits were killed one Sunday morning, following on from the deaths of ten rabbits the month before, while a total of twenty-two rabbits were killed at two elementary schools in the same month. Since the method of dispatching the bunnies was the same – the killer appeared to trample or squeeze them to death, leaving them with broken ribs and crushed hearts – police think the cases are linked.

An unknown bird hater shot and killed seventy-three protected kittiwakes nesting in cliffs in Marsden Bay, Tyneside, then laid them out two deep on a pub courtyard at the foot of the cliffs to spell out the word 'death'.

An Oregon man, Brian Raymond Rowe, was perhaps trying to prove his archery skills, or maybe his cool assassin's temperament. Either way, when he chose to kill two of his neighbour's Labrador retrievers with a bow and arrows he was sentenced to nineteen days in jail.

revenge of the samurai

A German man named as Stefan S. from the town of Niederpleis vented his fury on the hedgehogs which he believed to have wrecked his garden by slaughtering them with a Samurai sword. Denying that the killings were part of a Satanic ritual, Stefan recounted how he halved one hedgehog and slit open the other four. He received a fine of 400 euros and had his sword confiscated.

Two cases of animal assassination in east-central Florida, USA, had a distinctly anti-establishment feel to them. First, a 10-foot-long dead alligator was discovered hanging from a tree, dressed in the green jacket of a state wildlife officer and with the name of a conservation officer pinned to its neck. In the same week an American bald eagle, the emblem of the USA and the only creature to be protected under its very own federal law, was found dismembered by the road-side, a mere 50 miles from the strung-up 'gator.

Some pretty strange animal killers were out and about in Montana, USA. Eight cow killings were reported in a three-month period, and they all bore a striking resemblance to a series of bovine murders that were carried out in the 1970s. Part of each cow's face, as well as its reproductive organs, was carefully and cleanly removed from the carcass; there was no blood, and predators would often not touch the body. Not only that, but no vehicle tracks or footprints were found nearby either. Spooky.

Angry at the excrement that some stray puppies were depositing regularly throughout the factory area where he worked, twenty-six-year-old Brandon James Ferguson dropped the four little pooches into a silage harvester used to process wheat, corn and oats, with obvious gory results. In court, co-workers testified to the fact that Ferguson had made earlier comments about wanting to play baseball with the puppies and tie their legs together so he could run over them. Despite

join the club

Norway's Fisheries minister, Svein Ludvigsen, proposed that tourists to Norway be offered a totally new experience: clubbing baby seals in order to reduce the seal population along the coastline. His argument was that licences to hunt moose are sold, and therefore it made sense to get holidaymakers to pay to help out the government. He went on to say that clubbing seals was fun and not nearly as messy as you might expect.

this, his lawyer described Ferguson as a decent, honourable man who simply made a bad choice.

Six racing pigeons worth about £1,000 were stolen from a pigeon loft in Boughton, Nottinghamshire ... but not for financial gain: they were soon discovered on a nearby footpath with their legs torn off and their hearts ripped out, with evidence of their having been tortured before they were killed.

The Wildcoast organisation has been tracking endangered sea-turtles for years now. One particular fifty-year-old turtle went out of contact when the transmitter fitted to it was no longer sending out signals. To the massive relief of everyone at the Wildcoast group the transmitter started working again and the turtle was traced to Magdalena Bay in Baja,

California. The only problem was, it was being barbe-cued. The $2,500 transmitter is still missing.

...BEING HURLED

Huw Kennedy, of Shropshire is renowned in the world of military reconstruction for his medieval siege engine. At 60 feet high and made from pine trunks, the machine is usually used to throw unwanted cars and pianos distances of up to 100 yards. But Mr Kennedy recently came under criticism from the RSPCA for hurling dead animals. Dead cows, several pigs and one horse have been hurled 'impressive distances' with the sling. Some of the animals burst and splatter on impact, and the local children like nothing better, according to Mr Kennedy, than paddling around in the guts.

...BEING SPEEDWALKED

A Belgian man took his dog for a walk while he remained in the comfort of his car. The Alsatian ran alongside the car on a leash, pluckily keeping up pace as the car puttered along at 20mph and causing a traf-fic jam as cars queued up behind. When the driver was stopped by police, he said he was walking the dog like this because the weather was so bad. The forty-two-year old driver from Kalmthout was charged with animal cruelty. It reminds me of the old joke about the dog with no legs, called Marlboro ... because you take him out for a drag.

We all know how important it is to keep your pet well exercised, but this is ridiculous. A hamster was seen running along the hard shoulder of the M6 motorway near Birmingham inside its plastic exercise ball. Motorists alerted the RSPCA to pick up the hamster at Spaghetti Junction in Birmingham, and the little chap, named Roly by his rescuers, was taken to safety and given an extra bowl of sunflower seeds.

...BEING PLUCKED

In the Hungarian village of Buz-Czny all was not well. A flock of geese had wandered over the nearby border from Romania and eaten a field of cabbages. The villagers' revenge was to pluck the geese alive and drive them back across the border with an explanatory note around their necks.

...BEING FLEECED

Not content with regularly riding into town on the back of his sheep, Paul Jetsly of Ontario, Canada, also had a 'no smoking' symbol shaved into its fleece.

...BEING QUIETENED DOWN PERMANENTLY

The town court in Milton, New York State, ruled that a noisy rooster, Farmsworth, was in breach of local noise regulations by a few decibels. His punishment, on the advice of veterinary experts, was to be castration, which would curb his crowing instincts a little. The operation went tragically wrong, however, and poor Farmsworth died on the operating table, never to crow again.

Melinda Farren's ballsy tom cat Dollar would often come home after a night out with a note attached to his collar saying that he really should be neutered. Eventually, the unthinkable happened – Dollar went missing and was finally returned to his home in Rugby castrated. Police are treating the incident as criminal damage.

PETS EATING OWNERS

A concerned relative of lizard enthusiast, Ronald Huff, sent police to his apartment in Delaware after he had failed to arrive at work. On gaining entrance to Mr

WEIRD

bite your lip

Perhaps she shouldn't have indulged her darling poodle by regularly letting it lick her mouth after she'd drunk sweet tea, because when a woman from Warner Robins, Georgia, USA, awoke from an unusually heavy slumber (induced by a sleeping pill) one day, she discovered to her horror that one of her lips was missing. Police later found traces of blood around the mouth of her dog. Apparently Shorty, the one-year-old poodle, had also once stolen his owner's false teeth from her mouth while she slept. Skin was taken from the woman's buttocks to reconstruct her lip.

Huff's apartment the officers were faced with several flesh-eating pet lizards feasting on their owner's corpse. Seven lizards in all, the largest of which measured 6 feet in length, were taken away.

When Les Woodward went to stroke his twelve-year-old collie, Guinness, the dog turned and bit off part of his owner's nose. Les did not notice, however, that he was nasally challenged until he looked in the mirror and then spotted part of his nostril on the carpet next to the dog. His wife calmly picked it up and took him and his nose-part to hospital, where it was sewn back on. Les has no intention of getting rid of Guinness, but is seriously considering getting him trained. It seems that you really should let sleeping dogs lie.

...EATING EACH OTHER

Jerry Brown made an emergency call to police in Merced, California, to report that both of his pets – a burly, fierce pit bull terrier and a python – had gone missing. A search resulted in the discovery of the 14-stone Burmese python under the house, sleeping off possibly the biggest dinner of its life ...

...GETTING THEIR OWN BACK

Call it destiny, call it karma ...The annual pre-Christmas swine slaughter in a south-western Hungarian village came to a premature end in stunned silence after the death of a visiting Croatian man, electrocuted while trying to stun a pig. To add to this macabre turn of events, a local man who tried to unplug the home-made pig stunner also ended up in hospital with heart problems, and to cap it all, the owner of the pig was so distressed that he suffered a fatal heart attack. We don't know what happened to the pig.

A man from Stockholm, Sweden, usually got on very well with his neighbour's mongrel dog, but when he accidentally scared it one day, it snapped at him and bit his ear off ... then swallowed it. Attempts to get the dog to vomit up the ear failed, and by the time it was surgically removed, it was too badly damaged by stomach acid to be sewn back on. The man will now have to make do with an artificial ear.

A sixty-year-old fisherman caught a giant Spanish mackerel off the Great Barrier Reef. As he proudly posed for the mandatory trophy photograph, the fish, sensing its opportunity to spoil the moment, wriggled free from the fisherman's grasp, landed on the deck and ripped a 10cm gash in the man's leg with its dorsal fin. The fisherman was airlifted to hospital, by which time the fish was dead.

cats hate water ...

It all started when eighty-year-old Gerard Daigle of Quebec, Canada, decided to give his pet parrot a shower. It ended with four carloads of police, two ambulances and an animal control officer being called, and Gerard himself losing a pint of blood and requiring stitches. In short, Gerard's cat, Touti, was accidentally sprayed with water from the shower and went mad. The cat unleashed a savage attack on Gerard and when his eighty-one-year-old wife stepped in to save him she was attacked too. The police arrived in force to intercept what they thought was a full-blown domestic row only to find blood splattered on the ceiling, walls and floor, and the terrified couple huddled together having managed to chase the cat into the bedroom shutting the door after it. The cat, which had had 'a troubled past' was put to sleep. It was not revealed why Gerard was giving the parrot a shower.

ODD

A chef at a restaurant in Cornwall was attacked from beyond the grave, so to speak, by a dead shark. Twenty-four-year-old Darren Smith was driving the 7-foot porbeagle shark to the Dolphin restaurant in Newquay when he had to brake suddenly. His hand became caught in the shark's mouth, resulting in him severing an artery and almost losing his thumb. Mr Smith's hand needed no fewer than seventeen stitches.

A shark attack is not all that unusual, not even the gruesome one in which an eleven-year-old boy's arm was bitten off as he played in waist-deep water off a Florida beach. What made this case stand out, however, was that a ranger was on hand to shoot the shark, allowing the boy's uncle to reach into the shark's jaws and pull out the severed limb, which surgeons then succeeded in re-attaching during an eleven-hour operation.

A man from Erfurt, Germany, trained his Staffordshire bull terrier as a guard dog. But when he did so he never intended the dog to chase him out of his own home. The thirty-one-year-old man had to make a run for it when his pet turned nasty and bit him, and would not even let him back into the house. The man is currently staying with friends in town while he ponders the dog's fate.

A retired university teacher, Diana Dick, from Oxford, died when her Persian cat scratched her leg, breaking a varicose vein and causing her to bleed to death. (Because of the large volume of blood in varicose veins, clotting sometimes does not take place.) Despite the attempts of her carer to staunch the flow and resuscitate her, sixty-year-old Mrs Dick, bled to death.

Divers off the Florida Keys have been sexually molested by a huge sea-turtle. The turtle, nicknamed Crazy Charlie, appears to have tried to mount about a dozen scuba divers, and since he weighs in at about 300lb it is really no joke being on the receiving end of his amorous advances.

It all went black for Andre Ronnlund from Sweden, diving off the coast of Australia. Andre and his companion had been followed by a giant grouper, affectionately known in the region as Grumpy. Possibly in the mood for a laugh that day, Grumpy gulped down Andre, leaving his breathing gear in shreds. Andre tried to force Grumpy's powerful jaws open, but failed. Just as he was beginning to black out from lack of oxygen, Grumpy ejected Andre from his mouth as suddenly as he had swallowed him, and Andre just about made it to the surface.

It was a bad day at the Better Beef plant in Guelph, Ontario, Canada (a euphemism for what would otherwise be known as a slaughterhouse) when one of the steers on death row tried a last-minute escape plan. As the slaughterhouse worker was about to shoot, it nudged the gun into the man's stomach at the exact moment that it went off. The thirty-five-year-old worker ended up in hospital, while the steer was turned into Better Beef. A nice try though, wouldn't you say?

INTRUSIVE PREDATORS

A Bengal tiger – clearly a great big pussycat at heart – wandered one night into a hut in the West Bengal village of Gosaba, where a farmer, his wife and three children were sleeping. They awoke the next morning to find themselves sharing their hut with a sleeping tiger, and promptly left the hut as quietly as possible. The authorities were then alerted and an animal expert came to tranquillize the tiger and take it back to the jungle. The experts' opinion as to why it didn't take advantage of a free meal was that it was probably very tired.

A happy camper in northern Queensland, Australia, became a very scared one, when he awoke to find a huge crocodile lying on his chest. Just as he realised what was going on, the reptile tried to drag the thirty-six-year-old man into the nearby river, but with the help of a friend he managed to escape its clutches, and was taken to hospital with nothing more serious than a few bites to his wrist.

ANIMALS GETTING TIRED AND EMOTIONAL IN PUBLIC

Sonja Arntzen, sixty-seven, from Krakeroy, Norway, was rudely awakened one day by a crazed elk on the rampage in her garden. First it wrecked her garden furniture, then trampled her vegetable patch before attacking her car. The elk then disappeared into the forest. Local hunters believe there are two explanations for the attack: the elk is either one that sustained brain damage in a road accident earlier in the year, or it was drunk from eating fermented fruit (a drunken elk had recently caused traffic chaos after gorging itself on mouldy apples).

Traffic backed up on a busy road through the New Forest in Hampshire when a New Forest

tears and trumpeting

When seven elephants were killed by a passenger train that mowed them down as they gathered on the rails near Digboi, in Assam, India, about a hundred other elephants quickly appeared from the forest and began to mourn the dead. Witnesses spoke of their trumpeting and shrill cries, and even said that tears were to be seen rolling down the mourning elephants' faces. The elephants refused to leave the site of the death of their kin, and it took six hours to disperse them and hoist up the train, which had been derailed in the collision.

BIZARRE

pony decided that he couldn't wait a second longer and began mating with a mare, right in the middle of the road.

A case of elephant road rage took place in the town of Eheliyagoda, Sri Lanka, when a bus slowed down and stopped in front of an elephant walking in the opposite direction. Furious at having its way blocked, the elephant proceeded to push the bus to one side and smash its windows.

BEING STRUCK BY FLYING ANIMALS

Ethem Sahim was engrossed in a game of dominoes at his local coffee shop when a cow fell through the roof and landed on him, knocking him unconscious and wounding his leg, which required seven stitches. The coffee shop is built into the side of a hill, where the cow was grazing, and when it wandered on to the roof, the roof caved in under its weight. When Mr Sahim came round he had understandable difficulty in believing what his friends told him had happened.

A trawler that sank in the Sea of Japan claimed to have been hit by a cow dropping out of nowhere, which most people would find unbelievable ... Except perhaps the crew of a Russian military cargo jet who had stolen a cow they had found wandering on a Siberian airfield and brought it aboard. The poor beast became terrified during the flight, ran amok at 30,000 feet and made a bid for freedom by charging through the plane's door. Just when they were passing over that trawler.

A runaway ram, pursued by eight farmers and two policemen, hurled itself off a 30-foot railway bridge in what Inspector Andreas Kirchtag of the Braunau, Austria police asserted was an obvious case of ovine suicide. The ram landed on a woman who was walking her dog, injuring her but not the dog.

Mike Madden, a part-time inventor from Huddersfield, designed a bird-feeding hat which he decided to road-test one day on a woodland walk. Mr Madden suffered a whiplash injury as he was hurled to the ground by the force of a nut-hungry grey squirrel leaping from a tree and on to the hat's feeding tray.

ANIMALS ON THE RUN

Think Bonnie and Clyde, maybe even Thelma and Louise: a Norwegian cow made a break from an abattoir and was joined in her bid for freedom by a bull. Together they galloped down a motorway, with fifteen men in hot pursuit. Several hours later they were finally cornered, and while it would be nice to say that they were allowed to graze together for ever, they were, in fact, taken straight back to the abattoir for the unfinished business to be done.

A giant African tortoise, Big Bertha, weighing in at 75 pounds, has a cruising speed of about half a mile a day. So when she escaped from the Animal Crackers Farm Zoo in Greenville, Michigan, zookeepers were confident that she wouldn't get far. Three weeks later there was still absolutely no sign of her ...

ANIMALS BEING GIVEN A HELPING HAND

It's well known that giant pandas don't breed like rabbits, to say the least (that's one of the reasons why their numbers in the wild have fallen so low). In the Giant Panda Centre at the Municipal Zoo of Chongqing, China, however, they get a little help. Panda Porn videos – footage of giant pandas having sex – has apparently reduced the number of impotent male pandas at the centre by 20 per cent.

Based on findings of research by scientists at the Rowland Institute for Science in Cambridge, Massachusetts, showing that fish can appreciate and identify different types of music, sharks at the National Sea Life Centre in Birmingham are to be serenaded by Barry White in an experiment to help them mate. Sultry songs by the Walrus of Love, as well as other romantic tunes, will be pumped into tanks containing dogfish, starry smooth hounds and tope.

Culum Brown, a researcher at Edinburgh University, hit on a way of helping farmed fish to survive in the wild. Brown believes that showing them video footage of one of their own kind being killed and eaten by a predator will teach them which fish to avoid outside the safety of the hatchery.

The South China tiger is very rare, with only forty-nine currently living in Chinese zoos, and fewer still in the wild. The problem is that in captivity they lose their sex drive, and in 2001 only one cub was born. So zookeepers in Chongqing are giving Viagra to a pair of tigers to boost their libido.

A zookeeper in Germany saved the life of a baby tapir by giving it mouth-to-trunk resuscitation. Baby Carmina was unable to breathe after her mother Conchita gave birth at Hanover zoo, so keeper Dieter Schulte, who normally works with elephants, took Carmina's trunk between his hands and tried to resuscitate her for several minutes. Soon after the baby started breathing, she was able to drink some of her mother's milk from a bottle. Zoo staff had been expecting a difficult birth because Conchita was only three-and-a-half years old, and tapirs, whose pregnancies last eighteen months, normally do not give birth until they are four-and-a-half. Dieter was given an extra day off to reward his presence of mind and first-aid efforts.

At the National Sea Life Centre in Birmingham a lobster was given her own radio after it was noticed that she tapped her pincers and waggled her tail when music was played over the sound system (the fish do love their pop music there, don't they?).

You would have forgiven astonished patients at a Blackpool hospital for having heart attacks when

milk and water

Comfortable cows are said to mean larger milk yields, which is why no fewer than seventy-five waterbeds have been installed by Farmer John Marshman in his barn in Syracuse near New York. He has noted that the stalls equipped with water beds fill up faster than those without, while Doug Ford, the bovine beauty sleep boosters supplier, confirms that when one cow gets up from a water bed another instantly takes its place; sometimes they even queue up for a water bed to become free.

they saw an 18-stone gorilla on a trolley, being wheeled past. The gorilla, a resident of Blackpool Zoo, had been ill for a while and was about to have a stomach scan!

Two turtles, Sly and Latina, were enjoying the sun on the balcony of their owner's flat in Wellington, New Zealand. Being curious, they climbed up a stack of tiles and promptly fell over the balcony railings, plunging four storeys down and into the back of a truck. Latina was killed on impact, but, incredibly, Sly survived. The truck driver found her bleeding and bewildered, and took her to a vet, who was totally amazed that the turtle had survived such a fall. Although Sly's shell was very much the worse for wear, with several cracks, and partially caved in, the ingenious vet managed to mend it using gaffer tape and glue.

...AND HELPING THEMSELVES

Apparently polar bears' teeth are very yellow in contrast to their brilliant white fur. No wonder then, that when a polar bear broke into the Svalbard Wildlife Service on the Arctic island of Spitsbergen it sucked out the contents of a tube of toothpaste. After thoroughly wrecking the camp, the bear swallowed some vitamin C tablets and made off, with fresher breath and a confident smile.

COWS WITH IDENTITY CRISES

Scientists at a Brazilian university trying to clone a cow ended up with a bull instead. The team at the

University of São Paulo believe that the cow may have jumped a fence and become pregnant by a bull in a neighbouring field just before being inseminated with the cloned cow embryo. Alternatively, one of the experts may have blundered and inseminated her with a bull embryo from their laboratory stores. Head of the team Professor Jose Antonio Visintin said: 'She must have cheated on us!'

Whereas in India, to the Hindus, cows are sacred beasts, across the border in Bangladesh they are no more than an excellent source of protein. It is estimated that India's Border Security Force kills hundreds of would-be cattle smugglers every year, while Indians who cross the border to get their cows back are held in custody. So the Indians have started issuing their cows with ID cards to make the nationality of cows near the border absolutely clear.

WHO'S A CLEVER DOG, THEN?

In the northern Portuguese town of Sobrado, there's a little black dog who has a very good habit. Preta, formerly a stray, walks 16 miles every Sunday to go to church, leaving her owner's house at 5 a.m. and arriving at mass in the neighbouring town at 7.30. She stands when the congregation stands and sits when they sit, and when mass is over, she trots home again – or accepts a lift in the car of someone she knows well.

A stray dog has been granted an official free travel pass after being a regular on public transport in Italy for three years. Every morning, Sadu, a husky, waits with other commuters for the 7 a.m. from Ostia Antica to Rome, and gets off 20 kilometres later at the first stop in Rome. He is a regular at a bakery for breakfast and a butcher for lunch. Initially, guards wouldn't let him board the train, but he was persistent and charming enough to win them over. Now he has his own boarding platform and the free pass came after Sadu went missing for a while and made a TV appearance when he returned.

When a regular player in a pub lottery in Epsom dropped out, he gave the spare number to his Border collie, Bosun. No one would have guessed that the dog would win the lottery three times, winning a total of £294. The regulars in the Amato pub aren't happy but Trevor Barker, the dog's owner, points out that Bosun did buy everyone at the bar a drink whenever he won.

Ross Lawson runs Lawson's Dry Hills vineyard in Blenheim, Marlborough, New Zealand, and he's discovered a great new way of finding out whether or not his grapes are ready to harvest: he gets his dog on to them. Tomi is able to tell which grapes are ripe and which are not just by sniffing them, saving Lawson considerable time by not having to use scientific testing methods. Tomi's talent was first noted when Lawson was measuring his grapes' 'brix', or sugar levels, and saw that Tomi only ever ate discarded grapes that were 22 brix or more – the perfect level for harvesting. Then he realised that she had been sneaking into the vineyards and eating the ripe grapes. So now Ross takes Tomi out among the vines and follows her nose to the perfect grapes to harvest. And Tomi is becoming as 'fat as a porpoise' on her rewards.

A shopping centre in Fife, Scotland, had to step up its security to stop a shoplifting dog. A black Labrador regularly stole biscuits and sweets from stores at the Glamis Centre in Glenrothes. The dog, who appeared to be working without a human accomplice, was even known to hide his haul in bushes when being chased, then return for it later.

Here's a little black dog that must have stolen a couple of lives from a cat. First, Sweetie was hit by a mail delivery truck in Park Hills, Missouri, USA, and presumed dead by her owner, Glenda Stevens. Glenda searched in vain for a heartbeat in the dog's body, and decided that Sweetie had kicked the bucket. So she dug a grave in her garden and sorrowfully placed Sweetie's body in it. Hours later, Glenda saw Sweetie's hind legs emerging from her grave ... A visit to the vet confirmed that the dog had a broken front leg and broken jaw, but far from being a zombie undead dog, Sweetie was indeed alive and well.

WHO'S A STUPID DOG, THEN?

Things went from bad to worse for a young couple in Missoula, Montana, USA, when they left their black Labrador tied to a water spigot outside their apartment, and maybe they got their just desserts too. The dog ripped the pipe apart, flooding their basement. The landlord had to enter the apartment to reach the shut-off valve, and discovered a marijuana-growing operation in progress. Police were called and found twenty-one plants, harvested marijuana, equipment for growing marijuana, a digital scale, pipes, rolling papers and what was believed to be LSD; the couple, Michael J. Staley, twenty-three, and Jenna Lee Fetters, twenty-two, were arrested and charged.

Autumn in the UK can be a very noisy time – the run-up to November the fifth, Guy Fawkes Night means days, if not weeks of fireworks going off every evening, as kids take advantage of the proliferation of fireworks. In Wolverhampton a man whose dog was rather sensitive to the noise, suffered a flooded home as a result. Driven crazy by the fireworks, the dog tried to get inside the television, then hid in her owner's bed, and finally attacked and bit through a water pipe. The dog was later put on a course of tranquillizers to avoid a repeat performance.

IT'S A DOG'S LIFE

These days we seem to pander to our dogs more and more: clothes, therapy, special food – all that sort of stuff. Here are a few more instances of man sucking up to his best friend.

Folk artist – or should that be 'folk artist'? – Stephen Huneck opened a church devoted to dogs in St Johnsbury, Vermont, USA. With its motto of 'all creeds, all breeds, no dogma', the church will honour the spiritual and utilitarian service to humanity that is given by dogs.

Don't you just hate it when a dog starts shagging your leg? Ricardo Brito, a pet shop owner in Rio de Janeiro, Brazil, announced plans to open a dog brothel, which, he said, would provide an outlet for dogs that tended to get off on human shins. Five bitches are to be put into service (spayed, of course), complete with red-painted claws to attract customers, and will work for fifteen days at a time in a back room in his pet shop. And, just to prove that dogs have it better than humans, the brothel's services are to be free of charge.

In the UK, Butlins holiday camps are something of an institution, to say the least. The canine equivalent, Muttlins, opened in Scotland this year, offering dogs a range of activities including canoeing, line-dancing, and treasure hunts. They can even have a massage with an animal physiotherapist at the luxury kennels in Anstruther, Fife. Owner Maggie McCabe provides packed lunches and afternoon refreshments for her guests and operates a bone-rating system in which five bones means a bed, permission to roam the gardens, and a dog sitter if they get lonely. Kirsten Donald, whose Border collies Jinx and Bree stayed at Muttlins, said that when she came to collect them they really didn't want to go home.

A new pet food received the seal of approval from rabbis in America. Kosherpets cat and dog food is produced from kosher animals, ritually slaughtered, and containing no dairy products. Non-Jewish founders Marc Michels and Martine Lacombe have been enthusiastic about the benefits of kosher products ever since they fed their own dog a kosher diet and found that it magically cured its eczema. The couple point out the many hygiene and nutritional advantages of kosher meat, which they say is

WEIRD

woman bites dog

Seventy-three-year-old Margaret Hargrove of Tallahassee, Florida, refused to stand by and let her little Scottie be mauled when it was suddenly attacked by a vicious pit bull terrier. Crouching in front of the pit bull the intrepid woman growled, lunged at the attacker and sank her teeth into it. The astonished pit bull lost its nerve, turned tail and ran.

processed in a way that inhibits the growth of bacteria. Marc Michels says that pets fed on Kosherpets are far healthier and less prone to disease. The Michels' business is doing so well that they have decided to branch out into foods for birds, guinea pigs, rabbits, parrots, fish and ferrets.

Tinkering with your dog's personality can have very unpleasant consequences as Chaddrick Dickson of Louisiana, USA, can attest. Dickson ended up in hospital having been wounded in his attempts to extract the gunpowder from a .22-caliber bullet by smashing its casing against the floor. He had wanted to mix the gunpowder into his dog's food to make the dog meaner.

CATS

A cat called Schimmy refuses to eat anything but Chinese takeaways. The seven-year-old cat's owner Sam Kinsy, eighteen, of Walsall, says it all began when she left a prawn chow mein and went to answer the phone. When she got back the chow mein was gone and Schimmy was purring with delight and licking his paws. Sam started leaving Schimmy a little dish of her takeaway each night, and within days he'd stopped eating his tinned food. Now, if she doesn't give him Chinese food, he gets moody and aggressive. Being a student, she might now have to get a part-time job in order to support her cat's habit.

homer to the sampsons

Homing pigeons that return over hundreds of miles are common, but homing cats are not so common. However, an orange tabby cat managed to find his way back home after a 350-mile journey across two states of the USA. With paws worn raw and ribs protruding, Skittles showed up at Charmin Sampson's northern Minnesota home 140 days after her family last saw him on Labor Day weekend in southern Wisconsin when they were packing up to return home to Hibbing, Minnesota. Now, well-fed and content, Skittles has settled into his old routine – snoozing in the living room armchair. **STRANGE**

ANIMALS ON THE BLOWER

Night-time phone calls from a heavy breather are always a little disturbing. But when, after three nights, this particular caller gave away his identity by letting out an unmistakably chimpanzee-like scream, the recipients of the calls knew exactly what to do. Chippy, an eleven-year-old chimp at Blair Drummond safari park in Stirling, Scotland, had swiped his keeper's mobile phone and was dialling out using the phone's number storage and redial functions. The park staff, who were the unlucky victims of Chippy's harassment campaign, searched the chimp's enclosure and found the phone hidden in some straw bedding.

A couple in Hornchurch, Essex, were aghast at the amount of their phone bill, but found it in themselves to forgive when they discovered it was because their cat had been dialling a racing tips hotline.

Caroline Laenarts of Belgium was plagued by nuisance calls day and night for over two weeks before it was discovered that the evil caller was, in fact, a cow! A mobile phone had been linked the cow's milking machine and programmed to ring if the machine went wrong. The errant farmer had, however, set it to ring Caroline's number by mistake.

BEING KIND TO LIZARDS...

A greedy lizard in a pet shop in Leeds was choking to death on a too-swiftly-swallowed locust until the pet shop owner saved its life by administering mouth-to-mouth resuscitation.

...AND BEING NASTY TO THEM

A woman who threw her pet iguana at a policeman was convicted of inflicting unnecessary suffering on the lizard but was nevertheless permitted to keep him. Forty-seven-year-old Susan Wallace had denied animal cruelty and assault, but admitted damaging a window during a fracas at the Anchor pub on the Isle of Wight. Wallace, known locally as the Lizard Lady, was asked to leave the pub after putting the creature, named

drunk in charge of a guinea pig

In Totnes, Devon, a woman was found so drunk she was barely able to stand up, unable to give her name to police – and she had a guinea pig with her. The guinea pig spent the night in the police station dog kennels while its sozzled owner spent the night in the cells.

Igwig, on the shoulders and heads of fellow drinkers. The doorman said he twice asked Wallace to leave, and that she threw the iguana at him twice. Wallace then went to the police station at nearby Cowes where she became abusive to officer David Harry and threw the iguana at him. It missed and hit a filing cabinet, falling to the floor. The 3-foot iguana, apparently recovered after which it spent a day at the Isle of Wight Magistrates' Court in Newport, reclining in a tank as testimony unfolded. Its colour was brown when a vet examined it a few days after the incident, which suggested that it was unhappy, but the vet agreed with Wallace's defence lawyer, saying that this could be because it was missing its owner.

STRANGE SURROGATES

Rambo, a dachshund became an unlikely surrogate father to a baby stork from the moment the young bird arrived in his garden in Neu Zauche, Germany, having been kicked out of a nest on the roof of another house by its parents. Rambo's owner Werner Staritz confirmed that his dog shared its food with the stork, named Klecks, and guarded her when anyone approached. The two animals were inseparable, even curling up together in a makeshift nest when it was time for their afternoon nap. The main problem for Rambo was the thought of Klecks migrating to Africa. Mr Staritz said the bird would have to be weaned off dog food before making the flight.

AND THE ORYX SHALL LIE DOWN WITH THE LION

A lioness in central Kenya baffled wildlife experts by adopting a baby oryx – a type of antelope that lions naturally prey on. The full-grown lioness came across the oryx in the Samburu Game Reserve, having scared off its mother. But then, instead of attacking the defenceless calf, the lioness adopted the baby, protecting it from other predators, including cheetahs. It was thought that the lioness had not yet mothered any babies herself. Extraordinarily, the lioness still allowed the mother oryx occasionally to come and feed her calf before chasing her away. The lioness would lie down to rest in the afternoon with her unlikely charge curled up beside her.

Ultimately, however, the law of the jungle prevailed. The lioness had led the oryx to the river to drink, and, exhausted by two weeks of looking after her adopted baby, she fell asleep. While she slept, a hungry male lion in the area wasted no time in helping himself to an easy meal.

In an amazing postscript to this episode – some would say too amazing to be true – the same lioness later adopted a second, and then a third oryx calf. Cynics believed that even if the first incident was genuine, the second and third could only have been the result of opportunism on the part of those who stood to benefit from the hugely increased tourist traffic to the game park; in other words, they were staged. Believers, on the other hand, felt that if the lioness could adopt one oryx, and suffer its loss, she could adopt again. Kenyan tourism minister Kalonzo Musyoka was philosophical about the matter. He said the tale might have a spiritual connotation, because the Bible foretold that the lion and the lamb would lie together.

THE BIRDS

On returning home from holiday, a woman from Chongqing City in China was astonished to hear her pet mynah bird uttering words like, 'I love you', 'divorce' and 'be patient'. The bird had been listening in on the woman's husband's phone calls to his lover in her absence, and was now spilling the beans.

In order to escape a £30 fine, John Lomax of Bristol had to take his parrot, Jake, to the local police station to prove the bird's penchant for shredding paper. Left on his own for a while in Lomax's car, Jake took the tax disc out of its holder and chewed it to shreds. It was only when police officers looked on as Jake ripped up letters on their reception desk that they eventually agreed to waive the fine, Lomax's innocence having been proven.

The electronic trill and tweets of mobiles are so common now that some Australian birds have been heard to imitate them. Apparently, the birds use the sounds as part of their mating and territorial rituals, and when a male produces a new sound it shows he is up to date and hence a desirable mate.

Two robbers were arrested because of an exploding crow. A resident of Rock Forest, Quebec, Canada, called police when he heard an unusually loud bang at the local electricity substation. Investigating officers came to check out the noise, which turned out to have been a crow flying into the substation and exploding – and while they were there they noticed a bag of cash stolen from a local bank, and were able to trace the robbers and arrest them. Lucky police, unlucky crow and unlucky robbers.

A parrot from Rochdale that found itself being stalked by neighbourhood cats learned to bark like a dog. End of problem.

A police officer in Vancouver, Canada, was stopped on the street by a mother wanting help to find her children. The mother in question was a duck,

very creepy crawlies

Having attended several patients exhibiting highly unusual symptoms (including nephritis) after being bitten by spiders, doctors in Barnaul, a town in Kazhakstan, concluded that a mysterious strain of mutant black widow spiders was at large. The local poisonous spider, the karakurt, would not have been responsible for these symptoms, and when sanitary inspectors eventually caught several specimens of the rogue spiders they were pronounced to be like the black widow, but bigger.

WEIRD

who pulled at Ray Petersen's trouser leg until he followed her to a sewer grating. When he tried to walk away she again grabbed his leg, then went to lie on the grating. Persuaded eventually to take a look, Petersen saw eight ducklings that had fallen between the bars and were trapped below. Petersen arranged for a tow truck to lift the grating, and the ducklings were rescued one by one using a colander.

A postman delivering letters to Weymouth Mews, an exclusive London street, became the victim of regular assaults by lesser black-backed gulls living on the roof of number 33. Apparently driven to attack people with bald or shiny heads, the gulls eventually forced the postman to deliver the Weymouth Mews mail to a nearby street, and residents had to pick up their mail from there.

PLANET OF THE APES

In the German town of Zinnwald-Georgenfeld, police had to deal with a beastly crime: a monkey jumped on a man's chest, rifled his pockets and made off with his cash. The evil mastermind behind the theft appeared to be a twelve-year-old boy, seen earlier holding the monkey, who ran off after the monkey once it had secured the money.

It must have borne a strong resemblance to a family member – that's probably why a male monkey rushed up to twenty-four-year-old Rosmani

baboon burglary

Hundreds of terrified women fled their homes in Swaziland to take refuge in towns, after a series of attacks by baboons. The attacks took place at night, the baboons, talking among themselves in English and jumping on the roofs of single women's homes demanding sex and food, and stealing livestock. Swazi parliament had passed a motion to have all baboons exterminated before police investigators made an important breakthrough: that baboons cannot speak, let alone speak English. Lying in wait for the marauding primates their hunch paid off: the baboons turned out to be three youths wearing stolen ceremonial baboon skins.

Liawati Sheri and snatched her baby from her breast. The monkey escaped from the house, in Kota Baharu, Malaysia, and tried its damnedest to hold on to the baby, even when it was cornered by Rosmani and her three sisters-in-law. It took ten minutes of tugging and wrestling before they finally got the baby (completely unmoved by all the fuss) back.

In the summer of 2001, New Delhi, India's capital was gripped by terror. Dozens of people reported that they had been bitten or clawed by the Monkey Man, and at least three people fell to their deaths from buildings, convinced the Monkey Man was chasing them. At the height of the panic, vigilante groups armed with sticks patrolled the streets at night on the lookout for the creature and police announced a reward for information leading to its capture. They received nearly 350 alerts of Monkey Man sightings or attacks, but the phenomenon was ascribed to mass hysteria rather than a 'metallic-clawed monkey creature' that roamed the streets. Still, two months later, well after the panic had died down, the same reports sprang up again, this time in the city of Patna, where a 'two-legged creature with a monkey face' was reported to have clawed a woman's neck from behind and run away.

DOGBOYS AND OTHER ANIMALS

Iranian nomads searched for three days for a sixteen-month old child, who had disappeared from their camp while the parents were working in a field. Eventually the rescue party found the child in a bear's den being suck-led by the mother bear. Medical experts found the child to be in good health.

Here's the classic Mowgli story of a child running with the pack unknown to the society around them. A Chilean boy abandoned as a baby was discov-ered scavenging food from garbage cans with a pack of fifteen stray dogs which, it is thought, raised and suckled him. The boy survived in the care of the pack, living in a cave near the southern port of Talcahuano, for eleven years. The boy, showing signs of malnutri-tion, leapt into the Pacific Ocean when police tried to capture him, having been alerted to his case by the municipality. An officer dived in to save him, and the boy was taken to a children's welfare society.

In the Transylvanian forests of Romania a shep-herd spotted a small boy eating from the head of a dead dog. He was completely naked and unable to speak. The child, now identified as a boy called Traian, had survived alone in the country's forests for years, looked after by wild dogs. Traian was underdeveloped and undernourished (despite being seven, he was the only the size of a three-year-old), but was expected to make a full recovery. When his mother, Lina Caldarar, twenty,was located, she said she thought her son had been adopted by another family.

Sport

In Italy, the frenetic medieval horse race known as the palio is not so much weird (despite the unusual clothing of the jockeys and the high accident level); it's more an old tradition. The 'Palio of the Goose', on the other hand, held in the northern Italian village of Mirano, was host this year to a gaggle of 120 racing geese. The handlers used sticks to guide their geese down the 419-metre course and the winner was a goose called Margherita, capably handled by eight-year-old Stefano Comacetto.

Everyone's good at something, and every dog has his day. So it should come as no surprise that there's a dog show that takes place in Newton Abbott, Devon, at which there is a section for dogs that can retrieve a sausage without eating it.

And talking of sausages ... Michel Vauvin, from near Bordeaux, won the pig-screaming imitation competition held during an annual pig festival in the French town of Trie-sur-Baise in the Pyrenées. Contestants had to imitate a screaming pig at various stages of its life – including just before it's slaughtered. Vauvin took the title from four-time winner Andres Farra to walk off with the prize of a whole pig.

iron-willed

A British team of four won the World Extreme Ironing Championships by climbing to 5,500 metres in the Chamonix Valley in the French Alps and doing a spot of ironing. Extreme Ironing combines the risk factors of adrenaline sports with the warm feeling you get from nicely pressed clothing. The British team who scaled the tricky Aiguillette d'Argentiere carrying their iron and ironing board, did their high-altitude ironing to beat off competition from a German who ironed while snorkelling off the coast of Malta and a South African BMX-ironing duo.

With Britain in the grip of the foot-and-mouth disease crisis, the Scottish Wool Centre, in Stirlingshire, Scotland, had to give up its sheepdog displays – well at least those involving sheep. The National Dog and Duck Championships were set up instead, at which sheepdogs herded ducks, 50-metre races for the ducks were held, and there was a posture competition to find the tallest standing Indian runner duck.

In the World Pea Throwing Championships 2001, held in Lewes, East Sussex, the winner was local competitor Mike Deacon. He managed to throw a single frozen pea 44 metres, easily beating the previous record of 29 metres.

This may or may not count as sport, but it's impressive whatever it is (and if it's true!). Chinese Wang Chuntai, who has been building up his eyelids for the last twenty years, reportedly pulled a 1.5-ton car a distance of 14.5 metres in south-west China's Sichuan Province using two Z-shaped hooks which he tied to a rope on the car. He was hoping to have his feat recognised as a world record. He apparently has also used his eyelids to lift and carry an eight-year-old girl weighing 30.5 kilograms for eight seconds.

Power juggling – now there's a real man's sport. Milan Roskopf of the Slovak Republic beat his own power juggling world record by juggling three balls for seven minutes and seven seconds. The balls each weighed 6½ pounds, and Milan made 180 throws a minute, meaning that the combined weight of the balls during the time he was juggling them was 8,300 pounds. This took place, by the way, during the 4th Slovak Juggling Championships – there are, as yet, no international power juggling competitions.

sink or swim attempt

A Romanian has been training for ten years to gain entry to the *Guinness Book of Records* by becoming world record holder for swimming with his arms and legs tied and now feels he is ready. He also stated that he wanted to enter the Guinness Book for hanging by the neck for 90 seconds.

ODD

When UEFA officials went to visit the Stadium of Ankara, home to the Turkish football club Genclerbirligi, to carry out a routine stadium inspection, they made a rather strange discovery. The stadium had been surreptitiously hooked up to the city's electricity supply using a link that had been put in sixty-five years previously; as a result the club had not paid a single power bill since 1936. After the inspection the club promised it would start paying for its electricity.

A greyhound, who must for betting reasons remain nameless, had a career revival. An examination following a long losing streak revealed that the dog was extremely short-sighted, and was concentrating on getting round the track by running behind the leader. Pip Boydell at the Animal Medical Referral in Manchester fitted the greyhound with contact lenses and the dog, who was suddenly able to see the hare, started to win races.

Is it a sport or just a passing fad? Only time will tell, but in New Zealand, home to many extreme sports, wheelie-bin racing has become a hot craze. Drivers attach the bins to the backs of their cars and see who can drive farthest or fastest before the bin shatters. Bins have been found wrecked several kilometres from their homes and police are now concerned that it won't be long before races are held with someone riding in the bin.

TOUCHING MOMENTS IN SPORT

Rugby League is a tough game at the best of times, and nowhere is it played harder than in Australia. Wests Tigers winger John Hopoate, however, put more into his defensive tackling than normal and was suspended for twelve weeks having being found guilty of poking his fingers up the anuses of three North Queensland players. The charge was 'unsportsmanlike interference' and video evidence made his guilt clear. In a fairly predictable end to this story, Hopoate scored a try on his return from the ban and immediately bared his buttocks to the crowd.

Not strictly a sports story, this one, although it does concern a game, and goes so very nicely with the last one ... There has been a surge of popularity in Japan for a new arcade game called Boong-Ga Boong-Ga in which the player picks a hated victim

cock and ball story

Footballer Jose Antonio Reyes scored a goal for Sevilla in their 4-0 win over Valladolid in Spain's Primera Liga, and was congratulated by teammate Francisco Gallardo in a highly unorthodox way. Video evidence confirmed that Gallardo had bent down and nibbled at the goalscorer's genitals. Just his little way of saying 'well done'.

(ex-boyfriend or con man, for example) and gets to poke a huge (and virtual) finger up their clothed bottom. The harder they go at it, the more pain shows in the victim's expression.

HELPING THE OPPOSITION BY INJURING YOURSELF

In American football, Arizona Cardinals' placekicker Bill Gramatica kicked his sixteenth field goal of the year in twenty tries, against the Giants, leaped into the air in celebration, and ruptured his anterior cruciate ligament as he landed, ending his season and putting his whole career as a kicker (for American football is so specialised that kicking is all that he does) in serious jeopardy.

Football is taken very seriously in Argentina; and that includes celebrating a goal. In the Copa del Rey game between Villareal and Levante, Villareal's Argentine international, Martin Palermo, scored in extra time, then, celebrating in style, he leapt on to a low wall by the side of the pitch and beckoned supporters to join him. The wall crumbled under the weight and collapsed, fracturing Palermo's ankle in the process.

Love & Marriage

From proposing to his girlfriend to marrying her took New Zealander Russell Wilson just one hour. The thirty-nine-year-old secretly planned the wedding and the reception, invited eighty guests, then gave his girl-friend, Raewyn Turley, fake invitations to a ball. Just before leaving for the 'ball' he proposed and got the 'yes' he was confidently expecting.

Leanne Redmond's ex-husband was getting married again and it was just all too much for her.

bang-up celebrations DAFT

It was a traditional Turkish wedding in the village of Cayla in Thrace – except that the bride and one of her relatives spent the end of the evening in hospital. Necip Cankilic turned up to the wedding of nineteen-year-old Safiye, and, as is the custom, fired his gun in the air (or so he thought) to show support for the newlyweds. Unfortunately, however, he shot the bride in the foot and her relative in the stomach with the same bullet. He later apologised for his mistake.

Leanne stormed into the wedding reception, found her ex's new bride and punched her. She was ordered by Wakefield magistrates to pay £75 in compensation and to attend a rehabilitation programme.

A Canadian couple decided to hold their wedding ceremony in a funeral chapel – after all, it was where they had first met and where their love had blossomed. Around two hundred guests piled into the Thomson Funeral Chapel and Crematorium to see Shane Neufeld and Christy McKillop tie the knot, although rumours that they would be carried down the aisle in a coffin proved to be unfounded.

Mattie Charlene Dyer is seventy, American-born, a teacher and speaks only English. She married Yang Yukun who's seventy-one, has lived all his life in Beijing, is a retired pipe-fitter and speaks only Chinese. They've settled in Canada. Mattie said the marriage was hard to explain, but that there was electricity and magnetism between them.

fundamental change

Life will now be a little more bearable for twenty-two-year-old Louise Bottom of Cardiff, as she's finally managed to lose her extremely embarrassing surname by getting married. Too bad her husband is Marc Butt though. (Maybe they should hyphenate?)

In Iran, a touching part of the wedding ceremony is when the couple lick honey from each other's fingers so that their life together starts sweetly. Bad luck for the twenty-eight-year-old bridegroom in the north-western city of Qazvin, then, as he licked his bride's fingers and choked to death on one of her false fingernails. He died on the spot, while the bride was rushed to hospital after fainting from the shock.

The rather uptight council of the town of Thatcham, Berkshire, would not allow a seventy-nine-year-old man to have his deceased wife's head-stone inscribed with the epitaph: 'A good mother, a good wife and a great lover.'

Twenty-six-year-old Sandi Canesco of Sydney, Australia, was suddenly widowed when her husband was killed in a road accident. She wanted her husband's remains to stay close to her heart, so she had hubby Dustin's ashes sewn into her breast implants.

A young Sri Lankan woman, in her early twenties, began an affair with a co-worker who as far as she was concerned was a man. After a brief courtship, they decided to marry, in a ceremony that they kept secret from her very strict parents. The couple lived separately for three months but then moved in together, and on the same day, the bride's parents came to the couple's new home to forcibly take back their daughter. When the twenty-seven-year-old groom later went to his in-laws' house to retrieve his wife, the parents became suspicious about his mannerisms and discovered that he was actually she. The unnamed bride had to go to court to try to get her marriage annulled.

In the town of Brasov, Romania it is a wedding custom to throw the groom into the air three times during the wedding reception. However, it is not the custom to inflict multiple injuries to his head and chest as was the case when guests threw one particular bridegroom up in the air but failed to catch him.

Mark Jaikeran, a prisoner on trial for murder in a courtroom in Trinidad's capital Port of Spain, was waiting for the judge to deliver his summing up. As he waited he stood up in the dock, turned to his wife and said: 'I do not know when I will get to do it again, so let me give it to you live and direct.' He then proceeded to serenade her with the LeAnn Rimes hit 'How Can I Live Without You'. When he finished, his defence lawyers and the public gallery broke into applause, after which he was convicted and sentenced to death for abducting and beheading a pig farmer.

TROUBLE AND STRIFE

Mircea Stoleru, forty-eight, came home drunk one night to his home in the Romanian town of Andriasu and fell asleep without making love to his young and beautiful wife, Fevronia. So incensed was she by this that she went and heated up an iron and burned her

GRUESOME

sea saw

A forty-four-year-old Korean seaman accused his wife of having extra-marital affairs while he was away at sea. So keen was he to stop her gadding about in future that he tied her up with a chain then sawed off one of her legs with a power saw. Police later found the woman's left leg in a nearby field.

husband on his right shoulder. Recovering in hospital, scarred but sorry, he admitted that he had been at fault.

 Twenty-two-year-old Amina Haruna filed for divorce on the grounds that her husband's penis was too big. However, the court in Gusau, Nigeria, ordered her to return to her husband, Malam Hassan Mujahid, after dismissing her claims that she suffered injuries when they made love. Doctors confirmed that they were able to have sex, and Malam said he still loved his wife.

A German man who was seeking sexual gratification in the red-light district of Aachen got his comeuppance when his kerb-crawling led him to his own wife, who, unbeknown to him was working as a prostitute. (So that was why she always had a headache.) Police were called to deal with the row that ensued.

Some lovers' tiffs get so wild they'd make your eyeballs pop out. In Munich, Germany, a gay

my lips are sealed

Newlywed Satyabhama Mugalkod found her husband's use of foul language during sex a little distasteful. She told her new husband Rudrappa how she felt, then rolled over and went to sleep. She awoke in the morning to find him huddled in a corner and bleeding from the mouth, having carefully stitched his lips together in an effort to solve the problem. He later had the stitches removed in hospital.

couple (aged twenty-five and sixty-nine) had a row which erupted into manic violence, culminating in the younger man ripping out the eyeballs of his older lover. Police were called in the aftermath when the younger man was seen walking down the street naked, while screams came from the older man's flat. His eyeballs were found later in the street, where the younger man had thrown them.

HOW NOT TO REACT WHEN YOU'RE DUMPED

A full eighteen months after his relationship was terminated, twenty-four-year-old New Yorker, Forest Simon, sent his ex-girlfriend a Valentine's day present that sent shivers down her spine: a plain black ring box which she opened to find his left middle finger.

In this story, the poor guy hadn't even been dumped – well, not quite – but the forty-two-year-old chiropractor from Vancouver, Washington, USA, could see the writing on the wall, and decided that a little attention-seeking was in order. You know the kind of thing: the cry for help that gets her running back into his arms, while violins play in the background and bluebirds flit upon the windowsill. So, when police went to his home in response to the girl's claim that he was continuing to harass her, they found the health-conscious former bodybuilder had disembowelled himself and was lying on his bed, with his shirt off, awash with blood and a quantity of his intestines resting on his stomach. He was rushed to hospital, but his condition was not found to be life-threatening.

ENFORCED CELIBACY

The women of Sirt, near the Turkish resort of Antalya, said nagging was not enough to get the men to do the work needed to fix up a supply of running water to the village. So they organised a collective long-term headache and banned sex until their menfolk did the work. The women who were genuinely tired of having to carry water from the well to their homes locked their bedroom doors and rejected all amorous advances until drinking water was supplied on tap. The husbands made a desperate appeal to local authorities to send the necessary equipment and offered their labour for nothing.

A Brazilian woman gave up sex for a year to try and bring good luck to her favourite football team. And no she was not a nun, and nor was she boyfriend-less. Twenty-nine-year-old Carolina Montebelo did have a man at the time of making her promise of no sex until Fluminense won promotion to the second division. And what's more, it worked. To her boyfriend's great relief Fluminense were promoted. That meant he got to sleep with her again and wake up every morning, as Carolina does, to the Fluminense club song.

Luther Crawford of Louisville, Kentucky, USA, has fathered twelve children by eleven different women, and was having trouble keeping up his child-care payments. In fact, he was in arrears to the tune of $33,000 and facing between one and five years in prison. However, the judge offered the fifty-year-old philanderer a deal: that he refrains from all sexual inter-course until the payments are taken care of. Crawford agreed, although later said that he thought it had been a joke, and that now he knew how to use contraception, he should be allowed to have protected sex. However, faced with a choice of jail or no sex, he chose the latter and was faced with the small matter of telling his current girlfriend that he was banned from having sex, possibly even if he was to marry her.

The King of Swaziland, Mswati III, banned single young women from having sex for five years. At the announcement of this decree, aimed at preventing the spread of HIV, he claimed that the country's chronic unemployment rate was leading to idle people occupying themselves with sex. The king, who had himself just chosen his eighth bride, a seventeen-year-old virgin, said that he would stick to his own ruling and not have sex with her for the next five years. The punishment for a man who breaks the new law is a fine of one cow – or £150 – which the king could easily afford, it must be said. In keeping with the new law, an ancient chastity rite was revived, in which virgins wear blue and black tassels to signify their status, while single women in relationships wear red and black tassels. Furthermore, young women are expected not to shake hands with anyone or wear trousers.

LOVE GAMES MISTAKEN

Drivers on a motorway near Schwabach in the south of Germany alerted police, convinced that they had witnessed a kidnapping in progress when they saw a blindfolded woman in the passenger seat of a passing car. A large-scale helicopter search ended in the car being located near a lake, and the helicopter crew descending on a twenty-three-year-old man who was preparing a romantic surprise picnic, lighting candles and opening a bottle of champagne, while his girlfriend waited (blindfolded) in the car.

In Denmark, a witness saw a man dragging a blindfolded woman into a forest and immediately called the police, who sent six patrol cars and a motorbike rushing to the scene. When police arrived they

ODD

he's shooting blanks

Police were called to a house in Hamburg when terrified neighbours heard gunshots, followed by loud, insistent groaning. When they entered the house they found a man and his girlfriend playing a kinky version of cops and robbers, in which he was shooting at her with blanks from a real gun, which had the effect of enormously increasing her sexual pleasure.

discovered the couple behind a bush enjoying the latter stages of their carefully acted-out sexual fantasy.

The neighbours of a bachelor in Munich, Germany, called the police when they saw him carrying the corpse of a dead woman over his shoulder. Armed detectives raided his flat to find that the murder victim was nothing more than an inflatable silicon sex doll. In fact, the man had a whole collection of them, and the 'corpse' that his nosy neighbours had witnessed was his latest flame, newly purchased from his local sex shop.

CONDOMS

The South African government was carrying out a census for which they were employing large numbers of people to carry out the door-to-door surveys. In a possible excess of zeal, each member of the census staff was issued with condoms as officials were apparently concerned that they might forget why they were visiting all these houses and start having sex with the occupants instead of filling out forms.

A group of explorers from New Zealand came up with a cunning plan to foil the infamous candiru fish that lives in the waters of Amazonia, where their expedition went. The tiny candiru, which is attracted to the scent of urine, can swim up the human penis and take up residence in the bladder, from where it has to be surgically removed. So the Kiwis took bumper packs of condoms with them to wear every time they went swimming.

An antiques dealer from Dundee, Scotland put an unusual part of stock up for sale: his collection of condoms, including sporting names like Phantasma and Neverrip, some of which are now sixty-four years past their use-by date. One of the packets sold by Alastair Jameson on the internet bears the legend: for tropical and Arctic use.

India's health minister had a problem with his country's sari industry: sari makers like to use condoms to lubricate the bobbins on the weaving machines since, it would seem, the lubricant on the condoms is particularly good at stopping the yarn from snapping. Wholesale use of the condoms in this way was, however, claimed minister C. P. Thakur, affecting India's population control programme, and he wanted it banned.

caribou condoms?

In the West we have funky things like strawberry-flavoured condoms; and at events like the Olympic Games condoms are handed out. Well take those two concepts and translate them into Eskimo, and you get around 15,000 condoms scented with the musk of ox, caribou and arctic char handed out at the Arctic Winter Games in Canada. Health workers decided to distribute condoms based on traditional Inuit animals after talking to teenagers fascinated by flavoured condoms.

A Brazilian condom company paid the leading football clubs a total of $1.2 million for the use of their crests on the company's condoms. But since on their launch day they sold over 3.5 million condoms, with Flamengo's supporters buying the most, they have cause to celebrate.

SEX TOYS

When sex becomes boring people often turn to sex toys to liven things up. Then they get bored with the sex toy, and things really start to get weird …

The checkout girl at a supermarket in Falun, Sweden, saw a suspicious-looking man with a large bulge in his pocket. Assuming he had stolen something, she asked him to turn out his pockets. For the man, it was too good an opportunity to miss. He whipped out a vibrator and pointed it at her (threateningly, as if to stab her with it, she was to say later in court), and asked her if she would like it in her. As he was to say in court later, it was a joke – or an offer. None the less he was jailed for two months for threatening behaviour, despite his reasonable claim that he was the victim, an innocent accused of stealing.

Buildings were evacuated and traffic stopped in Toronto after a woman, named only as Sue, mistook a vibrator for a bomb. She found the vibrator wrapped in black electrical tape and stuck to a length of plastic pipe in a café toilet. However, she didn't see the words 'Swedish erotica' on the remote control attached to the device. It took police less than five minutes to spot that the bomb was a fake.

When a pick-up truck exploded in East Haven, Connecticut, USA, fragments of it were examined by police to see how it had been made. They discovered that the device used was a pipe bomb constructed out of a 12-inch dildo.

Police were called by two horrified teenagers to investigate an apparent murder in Maine, USA, only to discover that the 'victim' was a sex doll. But according to police in the town of West Falmouth this was definitely not a joke. The way that the doll was bound in a blanket with its fishnet clad legs protruding and damaged to look mutilated, pointed to the 'crime' having been carried out by a violent and disturbed individual. The doll was taken for forensic testing to see if there were any clues that could lead to the identity of the perpetrator.

A German concept artist won permission to be buried with his latex lady-love. Karl-Friedrich Lentze, fifty-four, expressed the wish in his will. He said he wants a simple coffin, but doesn't want to be alone in it. Mr Lentze, from Bonn, was granted permission to be buried with his sex doll, but for environmental

cross purposes

You've heard of letters crossing in the post. How about lovers crossing? Ian Johnstone, of Sydney, Australia, decided to give his girlfriend a surprise involving champagne, flowers and an engagement ring. It was their fifth anniversary of being together and he thought it was about time. So, completely unannounced, he turned up on her doorstep in Ilkley, West Yorkshire (that's an 11,000-mile journey). The only trouble was, his girlfriend Amy Dolby had had exactly the same idea, and as Ian arrived in the UK, Amy was touching down in Australia. That's another 11,000-mile journey. One phone call later, and they were coming to terms with the fact that they had crossed each other in Singapore airport, where they had both been waiting for a connecting flight at the same time.

IRONIC

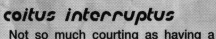

coitus interruptus

Not so much courting as having a full-on affair, a couple from Manchester were carjacked in the middle of a steamy backseat session. The couple, both tax inspectors, had covered the car windows with cardboard but left their doors unlocked and the key in the ignition. The carjacker got in and drove to Wrexham, Wales – some 60 miles away – during which time the pair got dressed with something like the same frenetic haste with which they'd undressed. Having reached his destination, the man apologised, gave the couple money for petrol for their journey back, and ran off.

reasons, it has to be made entirely of latex. 'Latex has got an awful smell to it,' said Mr Lentze. But as he pointed out, by that time it won't matter.

COURTING COUPLES

Dating through a lonely hearts column can be a risky business. Not, however, for the man who set up a date with a woman who, it turned out when they met, had been his first love at primary school in Hastings.

How long can you put off the fateful day of getting shackled to one person for the rest of your life? For most of your life is the answer, if Michael

fatal attraction

DEADLY

Sharon Carr and Robbie Layne met and fell in love at Broadmoor Prison, one of Britain's most notorious high-security prison hospitals where they were both serving life sentences. However, when each read newspaper reports about the other, in which Sharon was dubbed the Devil's Daughter after stabbing an eighteen-year-old to death at the age of twelve, and Robbie had stabbed and battered his mother to death and gouged her eyes out because he thought she preferred his sister to him, the wedding was called off. Their pasts obviously hadn't come up much during the falling-in-love process.

Beswick of Todmorden, Yorkshire is anything to go by. He finally married his fiancée Julie Gavaghan no fewer than twenty years after proposing to her.

A man from Hampshire made a habit of deliberately parking illegally on double yellow lines to attract a traffic warden with whom he'd fallen in love. Colin O'Neill parked in illegal zones near his home in Denmead for weeks to attract the warden's attention, having been won over by her uniform and strict attitude. He first met Doris Lemon, aged forty-three, when she gave him a £30 ticket for leaving his car for too long in a thirty-minute zone. The couple did eventually get married, but Colin will not be getting preferential treatment.

In a Cambodian double suicide with echoes of the *Romeo and Juliet* story, two lovers killed themselves, the second on hearing of the first's death. An eighteen-year-old former Buddhist nun was banned by her parents from returning to her religious life, and killed herself after the argument by taking rat poison. Ten minutes after hearing the news, twenty-eight-year-old Chhun Ouep, thought to be her lover, locked himself in a room at the monastery where the nun had been a trainee and also took rat poison, later dying in hospital.

Oscar Mntombo of Tembisa in South Africa's East Rand found it hard to accept that the woman he was courting was put off by him. In fact, when he propositioned her she ran home and locked herself in, at which Mntombo set her house on fire to flush her out. She ran to her neighbour's house, which he also immediately torched, and then on to three more houses, each of which went up in flames, one after the other. Eventually Mntombo was overpowered by villagers.

Serbian pop star Goca Trzan walked on stage, safe in the knowledge that all 4,000 tickets for her Belgrade gig were sold. When she went out on stage and saw just one man in the auditorium she burst into tears: a thirty-30-year-old Serbian businessman had bought out the show so that he could enjoy a solo performance and then propose to the star. Through her tears she continued with the show, and declined the offer of marriage, despite the chance of a one-way ticket to his home in Switzerland.

young at heart

The course of true love was blocked by police in Leon, in Spain, when an eighty-four-year-old man escaped from his old people's home to marry a girl aged twenty. The man, known only as Policarpo, sneaked out of 'La Corredera' residence where his young girlfriend was waiting at the gates. In a heart-warming twist to the traditional 'beautiful young bounty hunter marries rich old man' scenario, Policarpo has no income apart from his pension. His family witnessed his ecsape bid with some dismay and being unable to persuade him to return they brought in the police, who managed to get Policarpo back inside. His girlfriend, who is twice as tall as he is, had visited frequently, with nuns assuming she was his niece.

An American couple who had been going out for two years finally enjoyed their first kiss – at their own wedding. Katie and Tim McAfee, devout Christians, had agreed not only to a sex ban but also to no kissing before they walked down the aisle, in case the kisses lit some fires they couldn't put out, so to speak. The couple from Bismarck, North Dakota, prayed with their parents for God's strength every time they went out on a date. Tim said his kiss with Katie was great – but also pointed out that he had nothing to compare it with.

COUPLE CHEMISTRY

For some people the urge to merge is too strong to fight. It overcomes flimsy social conditioning in a tidal wave of lust.

An elderly couple was spotted in a steamy embrace at a Charles Dickens tourist attraction, in Kent. A member of staff at the Kent visitor centre spotted the pair in a passionate embrace but was too embarrassed to intervene because it looked pretty much as though they were having sex. It seems the pair had paid the pensioners' rate to get into the Charles Dickens centre. They then left before they could be intercepted.

Two strangers met each other in the waiting room of the hospital in Botosani, Romania, where they had each been taken with injuries from separate incidents. The fifty-three-year-old man and forty-year-old woman fell for each other while chatting as they waited for treatment, and shortly afterwards a hospital worker walked in to find them having sex. They both left immediately without treatment.

A couple at a holiday park in Cumbria were caught naked on cameras meant to monitor the movements of badgers. Despite (or maybe because of) the freezing cold and snow, the two lovers sneaked into the woods and began their romp, which was transmitted in every bedroom in the hotel on a special TV channel trained on to the badger sett. The woman kept her bobble hat on.

An elderly couple from York had to have counselling after arriving at their local church for an afternoon mass to find a couple having sex in the church porch.

A German kibbutz worker was in Israel's Ben Gurion International Airport, on her way home and with a few hours to kill. Described by the police who arrested her as 'a beautiful blonde', the young woman took off all her clothes in the car park and asked men if they wanted to have sex with her. One man walking through the car park took her up on her invitation, and they had sex between parked cars. Afterwards, the young woman carried on waiting for more men but before she could hook up with another one, a routine police patrol spotted and arrested her.

MARRIAGE DISAPPOINTMENTS

At least ten heartbroken Chinese men were cruelly dumped and left stony broke into the bargain by their brides. The ten men were each persuaded to hand over their life savings to matchmakers to marry the women, who all then ran off one by one – one 'marriage' lasted just three days. All the swindled men lived alone in mud dwellings on rural hillsides in the remote Changsha region of southern China, apparently without a hope of getting a wife.

It was revealed that the menfolk of the western Indian village of Bhoop Nagar were having huge difficulties in finding brides. That may well be because the contaminated water supply to the village causes the men to show signs of early ageing and to have physical deformities; it may also have something to do with the fact that the men of Bhoop Nagar are given to hunting and eating rats. The thirty-year-old head of the village (he looks forty-five) has a wife, but his father-in-law wants his daughter back.

JEALOUSY

It's not a pretty emotion. It makes people do things they may regret. Or, judging by what these people did, things that were intensely satisfying.

RIDICULOUS

you pig!

A husband accused his wife of flirting with the waiter when they were out for a romantic dinner to mark their first month of marriage. The row continued when they arrived back home at their house in Focsani, Romania, with the husband's jealous fit culminating in him stripping his wife naked and locking her in the pigsty. There was at least no other occupant in it, the pig having been slaughtered for the wedding feast. The wife, who did admit that the waiter was a cutie, was released the next morning by a relative, packed her bags and left.

There's jealous rage and then there's JEALOUS RAGE. Constance Kamundi, a Malawian woman, suspected a teenage girl of being her husband's mistress. She dragged the girl back to her house and forced her to undress. Then she rubbed pepper into the girl's genitals and wrote 'prostitute' in nail varnish on her forehead before driving her naked around town.

Agustin Garcia, forty-nine, could not argue with the accusation that he had shot and killed his former girlfriend on her wedding day. But he felt that the jury at his trial in Hackensack, New Jersey, USA, should be sympathetic to his situation. You see, when Garcia found out she was getting married, it was only three days since he'd last had sex with her. Good try, but he still went down for thirty years.

MAKING BABIES

A lesbian woman who was desperate for a child but couldn't conceive (of entering into a relationship with a man, that is) gave birth to a baby from a donor egg and her own brother's sperm. The unnamed American woman was fifty-one.

Jamie Cooper, sixteen, of Birmingham, is on the way to a sex change. But he has announced that before he crosses over, he will store some of his sperm so that when he becomes a woman he can have his own baby using a surrogate womb.

i'll just pop it in the post, dear

An inmate at a California prison won the legal right to mail his semen to his wife so that she could be artificially inseminated. Judge Barry G. Silverman said that forty-one-year-old Gerber, who is serving a 111-year sentence at Lancaster Prison, should be able 'to procreate from prison via FedEx', ruling that there was no potential breach of security in the transaction.

At a prison in Syracuse, USA, a female inmate apparently managed to get herself impregnated by her husband, himself resident at the prison, during the standard two-minute 'contact' visit. The woman was later heard to say that it only took them thirty seconds anyway.

A female couple wanting children no longer attracts comment. A deaf female couple wanting children must be less common. And the deaf female couple from Bethesda, Maryland, USA, are even less usual. One of them gave birth to a baby that they had conceived by artificial insemination using the sperm of a man with a long family history of deafness, so that the child would be born deaf like the rest of the family, including an older daughter. As it turned out, the baby boy is deaf in one ear, with the other ear having the potential to develop hearing.

DEADLY population boom

How do you single-handedly increase your town's population by 50 per cent? First, live in a town with a population of twelve, then give birth to sextuplets – simple. Sondra Headrick, thirty-three, and her husband Eldon, thirty-two, live in Rago, about 40 miles southwest of Wichita, Kansas, USA. Sondra was on fertility drugs, and conceived sextuplets, delivered by a twenty-four-member medical team. The babies were three boys and three girls. That sign on the town border that reads 'Rago: pop. 12' will have to be changed.

Bare Essentials

NAKEDNESS

Life can seem so much better when you strip off. Or weirder.

Two women students at the University of Maine conducted an elegant defence when they were up in court charged with indecency after they had been caught jogging in the nude. The law is clear that indecency entails exposing the genitals so the students asked the arresting police officer if he had really seen their genitals, and since, as the judge was later to point out in his ruling, a woman's genitals are mainly internal, he was obliged to answer 'no'. Case dismissed, and now women can jog naked in public without fear of police harassment.

Ninety-year-old Kanduri Bhoi of Tentulia village in Orissa India last wore clothes when he was ten and had a fever from a bout of chicken pox; every time he put clothes on his fever got worse, but when his mother made him stay naked he got better. Ever since, he has been convinced that wearing clothes will make him ill. Although local people understand his foibles, they do worry that some women might take offence, but his relatives don't think he could handle the pressure of wearing clothes now, so he'll be staying naked – and fever-free.

Gabriel Romanos has seen many psychoanalysts but they haven't been able to cure him of his urge to go running in the nude. And he's obviously a fairly fit nude runner, too. On his last outing in the town of Shepparton, Victoria, Australia, Gabriel was chased by

fourteen police officers and evaded capture for over two hours (adding resisting arrest to the primary charge of obscene exposure). Maybe after he gets out of jail he could get a job as a nude running coach.

A Dutch call centre advertised for nude workers in an effort to fill several vacancies. The advert, from a Rotterdam company, points out that it doesn't matter what you wear (or don't wear) in a call centre because the client can't see you. Naked staff would be provided with special chairs, and slippers and a bathrobe in case they need to go out. The company had a surfeit of clients, but a lack of workers to handle the business.

In December 2001, a forty-seven-year-old naturist announced that he had finally fulfilled his goal of driving 15,000 miles in the nude.

Leon Clayton of Bayou Blue, Louisiana, USA, robbed a store where he worked, stealing money, a telephone and some whiskey. The whiskey may have caused his downfall though: he was arrested a short time later walking stark naked down the middle of the road, and told arresting officers that he thought taking all his clothes off would make him invisible.

UNDERPANTS

There must be something special about the US state of Colorado and underpants ... Colorado House Bill 01-1221 became law, banning the wearing of aluminium underpants. Unless, that is, the wearer can prove that it is for a personal reason.

A company in the US state of Kansas developed magnetic underwear which, it claims, will cure haemorrhoids.

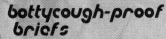

bottycough-proof briefs

Buck Weimer of Pueblo, Colorado, USA, came up with a great contribution to the world of underpants. Buck is the man behind Under-Ease, airtight pants which contain a charcoal filter that effectively, as he says, prevents the embarrassing odours of flatulence from escaping into the air. Weimer sold his entire first run of the briefs.

Following the advent of the euro, strippers in Italy have been issued with magnetic underwear so that their tips don't fall out. Whereas previously lire notes had been slipped into their knickers by happy punters, the same value now only exists in coin form, hence the need for something to keep the money in place as they gyrate.

Old Age, Death & Dying

OLD FOLKS

Wrinklies can be as weird as the young 'uns. Often weirder – after all, they've had more practice.

Sheila Cramp, a sixty-five-year-old blind grandmother raced around the Formula 1 circuit Brand's Hatch at speeds of up to 140mph. She did three circuits in an Audi TT Roadster to raise money for her church. Mrs Cramp had not driven for twenty years, yet she negotiated the course only with the radio communications of her instructor Peter Alexander. 'I truly couldn't see anything. I was concentrating on a voice telling me what to do. The G-forces were tremendous, I could really feel the pressure,' she said.

A US Chrysler Plymouth dealership sold seven cars, worth a total of $244,708, in a single month to a man with Alzheimer's disease. James Rickards, seventy-eight, of Portland, doesn't even have a driving licence. The dealership agreed to reverse the sales and pay compensation, and was fined $31,000 by the state Department of Justice.

An elderly Belgian couple's short day trip to a local beauty spot turned into a miserable odyssey through Germany lasting six whole days. Heading out from home to visit a waterfall, they hit some traffic diversions, got lost and unwittingly crossed the border into Germany, where, unable to read the road signs, they drove for six days in the hope of coming to a point they would recognise. They never did, but when they eventually broke down near Stuttgart, German police put them right.

At the age of seventy-seven, John Dreelin, a retired pharmacist from London, ran with the bulls in Pamplona's celebrated San Fermin fiesta. Although he was knocked to the ground, Dreelin made it to the end of the 100-yard run along with about a thousand other bull runners – for the thirty-second year.

The oldest stuntman in Britain, Ron Cunningham, decided it was time to call it a day. Cunningham, or as he is also known, 'The Great Omani', was eighty-six when he announced his retirement, and said he would mark the occasion by leaping on to a pile of blazing, broken bottles.

A sixty-eight-year-old Japanese man who could not stand the noise of the trains passing his house beside the Hankyu Line every day would rush out each time one came by and fire metal pachinko (pinball) balls at the carriages. He was arrested for wilful destruction of property after Hankyu officials said they had found more than 2,100 dents in carriages over the last few years. In Noriyoshi Nakayama's home police discovered pachinko balls, catapults and the Hankyu train timetable.

Several old people's homes in Denmark started showing porn movies in the communal TV area for their residents on a Saturday night. Since some of those male residents who can afford it apparently enjoy the services of prostitutes, it seemed the next logical step. Some residents think, though, that when you've seen one porn movie you've seen them all.

rip-off strippers

What is it about ageing Scandinavians and sex? At eighty and seventy-three respectively, Norwegian brothers Oystein and Arne Tokvam should have been sitting quietly in their armchairs, not inviting strippers into their home. The two men said they met two strippers in a shop (sounds odd – how often does that happen?) in the small mountain town of Flam, and invited them back home. The two women put on a show for Oystein and Arne in their living room, then said they needed to use the toilet, and went off together. They failed to reappear, and the brothers, on checking the house, saw their safe open and their life savings of £4,600 gone. They said later that they didn't mind the theft because it was the most fun they'd had in years.

SEXY

A ninety-five-year-old man has started growing new teeth. Nguyen Cong Du, a Vietnamese, had suffered the loss of his teeth over the last twenty years, but new front teeth and molars, 'as white as baby teeth' have been pushing through. He now has twelve shiny new teeth.

Eighty-seven-year-old Aubrey Offer of Keynsham, near Bristol, drove to his local post office and attached a bar-style lock to the steering-wheel of his car as he left it. When he returned he realised that he had lost the key to the steering-wheel lock. Not wishing to let a little thing like that bother him, Aubrey decided to drive home with the lock on, reasoning that since the road to his house was almost straight he wouldn't have to turn the wheel much. There was just enough leeway to allow him to drive to within a few metres of his front door, but then, when he tried to turn the wheel too far, the lock jammed, he lost control of the car and it slewed across across the road, crashing into the wall of a house.

Derby Goncalves agreed to pose naked for *Penthouse* magazine in Brazil. At ninety-four years old, the actress was a little older than the usual models but insisted anyway that the shots would be artistic.

Police in Taiwan urged an octogenarian prostitute to retire, after arresting her with a client. But as they said, with a little bit of make-up, Mrs Chiu, eighty-two, whose fee is just £5, could just about pass for seventy. So still time for a few more tricks, then.

Ninety-seven-year-old Gladys Adamson of Cambridgeshire had been virtually blind for five years when she came down with what she thought was a cold. She suffered violent sneezing fits that caused her eyes to run with what felt like boiling water, and a few days later she woke up to discover that she could see again.

For her hundredth birthday, Lady Morton, a well-known Scottish socialite, received a new car, complete with personalised number plates, and despite having had seventy-four accident-free years of driving she immediately drove it into a traffic island. Lady Morton was not hurt and said she had every intention of carrying on driving until her licence expires in 2004.

In a small bungalow in Sunderland, lived an eighty-three-year-old woman, Jane Potts. One day, a mighty gas explosion wrecked the rear of her house, one window being blown as far as 40 feet away. Neighbours frantically dialled for the emergency services and firemen rushed to the scene kitted out in special breathing apparatus. When they rang on Jane Potts's doorbell and she answered the door, it was for her the first hint that something had happened.

A Hungarian woman, Gizella Kosztor, had become notorious in the 1950s and 1960s in Hungary for a series of burglaries. Her modus operandi was to get cheap flights from Budapest out to rural towns, carry out burglaries, then catch the evening flight home. Aged seventy-five, released from jail, and in need of money to write what would clearly be a riveting set of memoirs, Gizella did what she knew best. But this time her usual airborne getaway was beyond her slender means and, having broken into several homes in a small town, Gizella was arrested at the local station, waiting for the next train home.

Eighty-year-old football striker, Kurt Meyer, won Germany's 'Goal of the Year' competition. He beat the efforts of all the professional players to net the prestigious prize with a spectacular long-range goal in a veterans' match. The goal happened to be caught on television and made him a favourite with the voters. Kurt has been playing for Blau-Weiss-Post Recklinghausen since 1971 and has no plans to end his career.

A ninety-seven-year-old man in Italy decided it was time to donate his entire collection of gay porn films to his local council. The resident of Rovereto in the north of Italy gave every tape in his collection to councillor Donatello Baldo and asked him to put them in the town's public library once he dies. The collection apparently includes 'all the masterpieces of the best gay porn directors'.

A German pensioner just couldn't resist the temptation to leave his footprints in wet concrete. But he didn't do it by half measures – under cover of darkness he covered half a kilometre of newly laid motorway near Berlin before road workers stopped him. Each and every footstep he made in the concrete had to be filled in by hand, and the man is to be responsible for the costs, estimated to reach as high as £15,000.

Talk about turning the other cheek. A teenager armed with a semi-automatic pistol approached Rita Walsh and Virginia Jakubajtys, both in their seventies, as they left their church in Boston, USA. The two older women's response was to inform the young man that Jesus loved him, then to anoint his forehead with holy oil in the shape of the cross. After claiming he was an orphan, he raised his gun again and got away with a handbag.

WHAT A WAY TO GO

Most of us would probably like to go peacefully in our sleep, having led a fulfilling and productive life, with hundreds of weeping mourners at our funeral. It's not always like that, though, especially for the people below, who met their ends in ways that may just have been more remarkable than the lives they led ...

A Romanian man died after choking on a filling while having sex with his wife. The forty-nine-year-old started feeling sick but his wife couldn't see what was wrong because their home does not have electricity (and, possibly, the noise he was making may have been interpreted as enjoyment rather than his death throes). Doctors confirmed that Marian Chiper, from Tiritu, died from suffocation after a filling blocked his trachea. Mr Chiper had had his tooth treated just one week before the accident.

Now we don't know for sure, but according to the evidence, a man may have hanged himself while asleep and dreaming. Michael Cox, thirty-seven, of Tresham had been a sleepwalker since his childhood and often dreamed about films he had just watched. Michael was found dead at home, hanged with his trouser belt, a few days after telling a friend he was going to watch the holocaust movie, *Schindler's List*, which has a hanging scene at its climax. Psychologists at the inquest into his death came up with the sleep-

fishing for compliments?

Todd Poller, from Iron County, USA, was trying to show his mates how clever he was. They'd spent most of the day drinking, and perhaps conversation had slowed down, or they'd got a little sleepy from the booze. Anyway, Todd decided to liven things up a bit by swallowing a live fish. Grabbing a 5-inch perch from the creek where they had been drinking, he opened his mouth and dropped it head first down his throat. Poller, forty-five, immediately began choking as the fish flapped inside his throat, and the efforts of his friends to dislodge the fish were unsuccessful. Poller was pronounced dead of asphyxiation on arrival at hospital, as well as having sustained severe lacerations to the inside of his throat from the perch's fins.

ODD

walking theory because there was no suicide note, and Mr Cox had apparently been planning a holiday with two friends.

 It's quite likely that Thai truck driver, Chotpan Sanuanpan, would beg to differ with the widely held belief that it's best to go quietly in your sleep – if he were still alive, that is. Mr Sanuanpan had fallen asleep face down on his bed, when some of his friends turned up to play a practical joke on him. They had brought along an air compressor, pushed the air hose up his bottom, and tried to inflate him. When the air began to flow he woke up with a start, then suddenly went very quiet. His friends took him to hospital and fled before the police could get involved, while Mr Sanuanpan, whose insides were ruptured by the compressed air, died soon afterwards. Some joke.

An Italian man, Andreas Plank, was hoping to get £300,000 in an insurance fraud and share the money with his cousin, but it all went horribly wrong. The plan was this: Andreas's cousin cuts off Andreas's leg with a chainsaw and makes his getaway, while Andreas phones the hospital on his mobile, is nursed back to health and makes a tidy £300,000 profit. Twenty-three-year-old Andreas bled to death and died almost instantly; all the telephone operator heard was 'a deep sigh then nothing else'.

A resident of Springfield, Ohio, USA, returned home to see a strange truck parked outside his house. Steve Lowry entered his home cautiously and saw a figure sprawled in the hallway. He shouted at the man, who didn't answer because he was dead, then ran to a neighbour for help. The dead man, fifty-four-year-old Robert H. Miller, had been burgling Mr Lowry's house, having already done over another house in the vicinity. But he got his comeuppance in Mr Lowry's house when he suffered a fatal heart attack. Miller's truck was found to have over £10,000 worth of imported figurines stashed in it.

SUICIDE STORIES

Life can be hard. And, ironically, it can be hard on those who try to end it.

A Berlin man decided the best way to end it all would be to make his way to the Friedrichsfelde nature park in east Berlin (having downed a bottle of plum brandy for Dutch courage), climb a fence, then scale a wall to get into the bear enclosure, strip naked and let himself be eaten alive by the three brown bears. However, three well-fed, happy and incurious bears – as it turned out, that is – ignored him despite his entreaties to them to eat him. Police pulled him out, referring to him rather unkindly as 'Goldilocks'.

A woman in Shawnee County, USA, tried to kill herself, failed, and on regaining consciousness dialled 911 for the emergency services before passing out again. When rescue workers arrived, they saw her

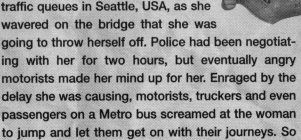

you're making us late for work

A suicidal woman caused three-hour traffic queues in Seattle, USA, as she wavered on the bridge that she was going to throw herself off. Police had been negotiating with her for two hours, but eventually angry motorists made her mind up for her. Enraged by the delay she was causing, motorists, truckers and even passengers on a Metro bus screamed at the woman to jump and let them get on with their journeys. So she did. She didn't die though and ended up in hospital with spinal, chest and abdominal injuries.

and, assuming she was dead, cancelled the ambulance that was on its way to save her life. With workers standing outside the house to protect it as a crime scene, the woman came round once more, and again called 911. The call was transmitted to the rescue workers outside the house and this time they rushed inside to give medical aid. She eventually made it to hospital in reasonable shape.

In Los Angeles, USA, one thing led to another as a twenty-eight-year-old man shot and killed his wife, then drove to a highway overpass and shot and killed himself, as a result of which he fell over the railings and on to a Toyota Camry killing the driver.

A man in Nashville plummeted off a hotel balcony. Having strangled his wife, he was pushing her off the balcony and followed through a bit too far, losing his balance and clumsily engineering his own death as he did so.

A Thai man tried to commit suicide by swallowing nails. It took twenty-seven-year-old Sommai Kaiwinit several hours to realise that having swallowed more than 100 nails without drinking any water he was not going to die. Next, he climbed to the top of an electricity pylon and jumped. Miraculously, or unfortunately, depending on your viewpoint, Mr Kaiwinit survived the drop and was found by villagers in the morning. Doctors said they would operate to remove the nails from his stomach but the injuries from the fall were so severe that he might never walk again.

A farmer in China had surgery for a detached retina. But Bao Jihou was so frustrated by the failure of the operation to restore his sight that he went to the hospital in Chongqing and blew himself up with a home-made bomb, making sure he also killed the doctor who had carried out the surgery.

The Swedish furniture company IKEA occasionally runs some unusual advertising campaigns. One that didn't go down very well in Germany, provoking strong reactions from police and press, featured a glum gnome laying its head on a railway line, while the caption encouraged people not to be depressed because IKEA had come to town. Police in Regensburg were particularly incensed, saying the ad made light of suicide. It was removed from sites near railway lines, where, according to Police Officer Hans Rachwalik, in the previous six months seventy people had lain down on the tracks, forty-eight of whom had died. Iris Skowronek, Campaign Executive for IKEA in Regensburg was of the opinion that the ad had been misinterpreted.

You can never be sure about what will drive a man to take his own life, but you wouldn't have guessed that defending the honour of TV picture quality would figure highly as a motive. Nevertheless, that's what happened in Amsterdam, home of Philips Electronics. A protesting man shot himself to death after an eighteen-hour hostage stand-off because he was upset at misrepresentations about the quality of 16 x 19-inch television screens.

BREAKING UP IS HARD TO DO

When a loved one dies, most people arrange a funeral. It's sad, but natural, and it's a way of saying goodbye to the deceased. The people below, however, don't come into the 'most people' category and they found it particularly hard to say goodbye …

Two women shared a house in Dewsbury and the younger of the two, forty-two-year-old Marie Walton, suffered with a stomach complaint. However, the speed of her passing took her seventy-three-year-old companion, Betty Freeman, totally by surprise. Marie went to lie down in the lounge, saying she wasn't feeling well; the next thing Betty knew, Marie was dead. Stunned, panicked and confused, Betty took the path of least resistance and simply left the body where it was. As each day passed it became harder for her to tell anyone about it, until, after four months of co-existence with the corpse, Betty was visited by the social services, alerted by neighbours. The game was up and the partly mummified body of Marie, hidden beneath a huge pile of clothes, was removed.

A Chilean man killed his lover, supposedly in a row over household chores, and then went on sleeping next to the corpse for the next forty-five days. The murdered lover's body was found in an advanced state of decomposition in the couple's bed by police after a visit from the victim's sister aroused her suspicions – the murderer told her that her brother – his lover – had suddenly moved away.

Two sisters in Santiago, Chile, were found sharing an apartment with their dead mother and thirty cats. Officials calling at the flat in Santiago discovered the women sharing a mattress with the body of their mother, Flor Nunez, eighty-six, who had been dead for at least four days. The two sisters, Elena and Ernestina Nunez, aged sixty-five and forty-two, had decided not to inform the authorities about the death because they wanted to carry on living normally. If living with a dead

you may now leave the table

In Pokrovsk, Russia, a man lived with his dead flat-mate sitting upright at the table, fork in hand, for a full week. The dead man slipped away to the great kitchen in the sky during lunch, and continued sitting with his eyes open (perhaps the service at lunch had been a little slow). Anyway, the dead man's flatmate had no money to bury him and the council refused to move an 'ownerless' body. Soldiers eventually broke the deadlock and did the tidying up.

body and thirty cats in a small and very smelly apartment can be called normal, that is.

Police in the town of Vancouver in the state of Washington, USA, found that a woman had been living with her eighty-six-year-old mother's dead body for five months. The pair shared a flat, and when her mother died, the daughter told police that she had been unable to come to terms with the death and so had told nobody.

Here's a spin on the 'Princess and the Pea' fairy tale (in which the princess detects the presence of a pea under a mattress and gets to marry the prince because she is clearly true princess material). The twelve women in this story who used a love hotel in Kyoto over a period of several days clearly had no princess potential since they failed to notice that under the mattress of their hotel bed was a body of a dead woman. They and their male partners made love on a mattress which 'had a few bumps in it', to which they paid no attention (well, they did have other things on their mind). The chambermaid finally spotted the body, which had started to bloat, making the lumps bigger, when she was changing the sheets. A murder investigation duly ensued.

There are only two legal ways to dispose of a dead body in France: burial and cremation. Placing the body of your wife, who has died of cancer, in a refrigeration system in the basement of your house

frozen father

An unemployed Japanese man from Yokohama had a rather shaky grasp on basic biology, or maybe a faith bigger than Mount Fuji. When his father died, he put his body in a large freezer, thinking that one day 'the cells would revive'. The body stayed there, not showing the slightest sign of reviving, for thirteen years, until the man's electricity was cut off due to non-payment of bills. The corpse then thawed, of course (but still no signs of revival), and a terrible smell coming from the man's home soon caused the neighbours to complain to the police.

in the hope that future medical advances will allow her to be resurrected, therefore, is not legal. This is what Dr Raymond Martinot did in 1984, and when he died at the age of eighty, eighteen years later, he had himself placed next to her. Before his death he had regularly guided visitors around the basement complex, showing off the equipment that would one day help him and his wife to live again. When local authorities found out, however, they declared it a clear breach of regulations, and ordered that both bodies be thawed and disposed of properly, totally scuppering the couple's chances of having their lives back one day in a new age of medical technology.

MY TIME'S UP

Knowing when to leave is the mark of the perfect guest. Knowing when your time on earth is up shows sensitivity too.

Harold Saber, eighty, was described as a quiet man, who didn't like to bother anybody. The retired pharmacist from New Jersey, USA, had a long history of illness and when he was seventy he made financial arrangements for his funeral, whenever that should be.

One day, without a word to anyone, he drove himself to the funeral home and died at the wheel of his car in the car park. Harold had always said that when it was 'his time' he would get himself to the funeral parlour.

A perfectly healthy Romanian man bought a grave and a cross which he had inscribed with the year he predicted that he would die. Seventy-year-old Alexandru Marin, from Branistea, Galati County, said he had had visions enabling him to calculate that he would meet his death in 2012. The visions included a cross in the sky in 1991, a big star in an unusual position in 1992, and a strong light shining into his house in 1997. Using these, Alexandru Marin chose 2012 as the year of his passing. 'We will see if I am right,' he said. Well, at least that much is true.

Work & Business Life

CORPORATE CURIOSITIES

Hasbro, makers of Monopoly, one of the all-time best-selling board games, were themselves accused in the

the sting

The American energy giant Enron Corporation went under this year, amid accusations of all sorts of impropriety and bad practice, with people implicated right up to government level. Among the absurdities of the case was the report from a former employee that the company ran a mock trading floor in its Houston headquarters, furnished with desks, large flat-panel computer screens and teleconference rooms. This hugely expensive sham was set up with the sole purpose of making visitors believe the company was energetically trading commodities at all hours of the day. The sad reality, revealed the employee, was that the equipment was only hooked up internally, and the 'traders' who appeared to be frantically placing orders, were just talking to each other.

SHAM

UK of monopolising the board games market through price-fixing. The Office of Fair Trading conducted a twelve-month investigation involving high-street shops and contacted several stores and companies informing them of the impending case. If Hasbro receive a fine, it certainly won't be payable in Monopoly money.

LGC, a British scientific analysis firm based in south-west London specialises in technical DNA analysis – hair, fingernails, skin, that sort of thing – and sometimes gets samples from employees to practise on. Recently, though, the request was for willing male employees to make their way to the men's toilets in Block One, make themselves known to the collectors and donate a sperm sample. The things people do for their companies.

TEAM-BUILDING MADNESS

Picture the scene: it's a business conference in Newport, south Wales. Delegates were enjoying their dinner when, to their horror, a group of armed, masked gunmen burst in through a window, firing machine guns into the air. Having allowed the diners a few seconds for the full terror of the moment sink in, the host then revealed that it was all just part of a team-building exercise.

A Florida, USA, production company came up with the idea of livening up dull meetings with acrobats and flying Elvises. The company, ME

grilled sole

More than 100 Burger King employees were burned as they walked bare-
foot over white-hot coals in a fire-
walking exercise designed to build
team spirit. Management had hoped that it
would help their workers to see that they could reach
beyond their limits and achieve what they thought
was impossible. However, the experiment ended
with about twelve members of staff being taken to
hospital with first- and second-degree burns. Some
flame-grilled employees were forced to use wheel-
chairs to get to the next team retreat.

Productions, feels that with audiences growing up on
MTV, more visual stimulation is needed than just a flip
chart to get people's attention. So they now offer illu-
sionists and jugglers as well as glowing spaceships
and the acrobats and flying Elvises.

THE EUROZONE

In 2002 the switch over from national currencies to the
single currency euro for most of the member states of
the European Community went quite smoothly, on the
whole ...

In Spain a reporter from an English newspaper
bought a pastry in a bakery and paid with a euro
coin. The assistant took the euro and, cleverly spotting

that it had been minted in France, tried to refuse it. Well it wasn't Spanish, was it? Her colleague quickly stepped in to save further blushes, reminding her that it was, well, the euro and that was the whole point.

Politeness and an appreciation for the currency of the future marked out three German muggers as a little different. The three approached a twenty-one-year-old man in Hamburg, threatened him with a gun and demanded 20 deutschmarks. The man produced a 50-mark note and handed it over. To his great surprise the muggers started sorting out his change – they had only asked for 20DM after all – which they gave to him in euros.

In Groningen, Holland, a ninety-one-year-old man bought a pair of underpants with Dutch guilders and checked his change when he got home. Of course it was in euros, so he returned to the shop and demanded his change in guilders. The cashier did his best to explain about the common currency, the euro and everything, but after two hours of arguing, the man was still thoroughly convinced that it was a trick to do him out of his pension. Eventually the frustrated cashier called the police, who, having likewise failed to get their point across, took him home and asked his family to bring him up to date.

Every eurozone country mints its own coins with its own national identity, as we saw in the Spanish story above. So don't opt for tails on the toss of a one-

silly money

Once the currency was in the hands of the public, many people felt that the notes had a slightly artificial feel to them, like toy money. A feeling backed up by the manager of a bar in Auch, near Toulouse, France, who was cashing up one night in the New Year to find that one customer had succeeded in paying for his drinks with Monopoly money.

euro coin in Belgium: two Polish mathematicians discovered that Belgian euros are more likely to land heads up when tossed. The large image of King Albert's head makes the coin heavier on one side, and in tests in which the coins were spun 250 times, heads came up 56 per cent of the time.

Adjusting to the single currency in Germany posed problems that had little to do with economic performance and rather more to do with sexual performance. A fifty-five-year-old German man, Wolfgang Fritz, was planning to sue his government, claiming that he was 'dead in the bedroom' and that he 'hadn't had a spark down there' since starting to handle ten-euro notes. And it seems as though he wasn't the only one: thousands of Germans alleged that the ten-euro note, the only one that is manufactured using a certain chemical, tributyltin, caused allergies and other ailments.

YOUR OWN JOB CREATION SCHEME

A US pizzeria manager was caught cooking the books in a big way. Kimberly Hericks, manager of a pizzeria in Cleveland, Ohio, ordered 400 pizzas then left them to rot in her garage. It was all part of her plan to boost sales and – oh, the price of fame – to get a mention in her company newsletter. She allegedly set up fake store accounts for local schools and hospitals in Ohio and insisted she deliver the pizzas herself to build a rapport with customers. Hericks, thirty-six, even tried to con colleagues by sending flowers to herself at the pizzeria accompanied by a 'thank you' note from a local hospital.

A Swedish company specialising in removing graffiti admitted to spray painting buildings to get work from the buildings' owners. The firm from Orebro came up with the idea of defacing local buildings when their workload went into decline in the mid-1990s. The company owner and his employees used to get drunk in the evenings and then paint the town red – literally – and any other colour. The following day they would contact the building's owner and offer them their services. Police eventually uncovered the scam after the company caused several hundred thousand kronor worth of damage to a building.

It's one thing to be proud of your sons, especially when they have chosen the noble profession of being firefighters; it's another thing to start fires to help them on in their career. An Austrian woman in the Styria region set several small buildings on fire then tipped off her sons so that they would be first to arrive at the blazes. After her sons' quick response to her first call, she set fire to her neighbour's garage, and let it burn a little longer in order to set her super sons more of a challenge. By the time they got there, the garage had burned to the ground. Over the next few weeks she tested her sons' speed and competence several more times until they became suspicious. When she was arrested, the woman said she was so proud of her boys that she wanted to make them look like heroes.

PAYMENT IN KIND

A Turkish soccer team tried to sell two of its players for 225 sacks of cement. Sarigol Municipality, who play in the first division of the Manisa Amateur League, had their offer taken up by local rivals Canakcispor. Sarigol were so delighted with getting their price that they threw two more players in as a goodwill gesture. Four players lighter, Sarigol were able to repair their stadium with the cement.

A taxi driver in Newquay, Cornwall, did pretty well out of his deal with a Russian trawlerman who needed a ride back to his ship in Padstow after a night on the town. The fare came to a hefty £34, which the man didn't have, so he went up on deck and came back with ten Dover soles with a market value of about £7 each.

tigers for technology

A government inspection of a zoo in Kazakhstan uncovered some naughty trading by staff involving the exchange of endangered animals for office equipment. One of the managers at the Karaganda Zoo managed to get a photocopier from a Ukrainian circus for two camels, whilst in another deal, two Bengal tigers and a wild boar were swapped for a fax machine, a typewriter and a fridge.

GENITALS
MAKING A MESS OF YOUR OWN ...

Mr Stefanescu, a thirty-two-year-old Romanian from Dolj, had a problem with his testicles. It wasn't that they were hurting or itchy or anything; he just felt that they were too big. So, he did what anyone else would do in the same situation and injected them with salty water. He was quickly taken by ambulance to hospital where he told doctors that he had once seen his father successfully use the same method on one of his goats. Well, he had thought, goat testicles, human testicles, no difference really. While walking was definitely a little painful, it was not yet known whether Mr Stefanescu's experiment would affect his ability to have children.

A sixty-three-year-old man from Lugo di Ravenna went to hospital with a severed penis wrapped in a sheet of newspaper, claiming that he had accidentally cut himself while shaving his pubic hair. Suspicious doctors informed the police, who went to the man's apartment and discovered that he had been fibbing. The man's vacuum cleaner bore traces of blood and a porn tape was in his video player. He later admitted that he had inserted his member in the vacuum cleaner and that part of it had been cut off by the cleaner's fan. He had then had the presence of mind to try and save the severed part in the freezer while the ambulance was on its way to pick him up. He underwent surgery to reattach it, but doctors held out little hope that it would ever work properly again.

A Peruvian man who last year chopped off his penis in protest at not having a job, has now sliced off one of his testicles because of low pay. Thirty-six-year-old Eduardo Velez Alejos had finally found work as a labourer after his penis protest (the penis was successfully reattached, by the way), but clearly this was not enough. The man asked guards outside the Peruvian parliament building in Lima to let him speak to President Carlos Ferrero Costa, and when they refused he pulled out a knife and cut off his left testicle. Doctors this time were unable to reunite him with his testicle during emergency surgery but said he could still enjoy 'a normal sex life'.

A Filipino, Rhudyll Isorena, was drinking with friends when they all decided to whip out their tackle to see who had the biggest. It would seem that poor old Rhudyll didn't come off too well in comparison with his better-endowed pals, and they wasted no time in telling him so. The twenty-five-year-old trudged home and, consumed by grief (and more than a little beer, probably) chopped off the end of his penis. Isorena, from Laguna, was rushed to the Philippine General Hospital in severe pain. Dr Jojo Castillo, of the urology section said that Isorena would still be able to urinate properly and that 'he can still have sex, although the thing does not look good'. The sliced-off portion could, it transpired, have been reattached but it was not with Isorena when he was brought to hospital.

... AND OF OTHER PEOPLE'S

Barrington Wynn, from Ontario, Canada, arrived home drunk one night and slapped his fifteen-year-old son. His wife, Donna, who could bear it no longer, grabbed his testicles, dug her nails in, pulled hard, and ... out they popped. While Donna was eventually charged with aggravated assault, Wynn felt he'd deserved it, and still loved her.

she's got balls (his)

Handing over a pair of testicles to astonished Chicago policemen after walking into their station, a forty-two-year-old woman calmly announced that she had bitten them off a man who had sexually assaulted her close to the HQ. The victim's victim, Erik Williams, was taken to a local hospital where the testicles were successfully reattached.

i had a little accident, darling

Police in Detroit, USA, tracked down a rape suspect from a trail of blood after his victim bit and nearly severed his penis. The thirty-one-year-old man ran home from the scene of his attack and told his wife he'd injured himself on a fence while running away from a dog. She then took him to hospital. Meanwhile, police officers interviewed the victim who explained that at the end of the assault she had managed to bite and severely lacerate the rapist's penis. They then followed the drops of blood to his house, found a large pool of blood in his dining room and called all the local hospitals to see if a man with a bleeding penis had checked in. They located him at the St John hospital and arrested him.

ODD

CUTTING OFF BODY PARTS FOR RELIGIOUS REASONS

A farmer in India sliced off his tongue to keep his promise to a Hindu goddess. Shambhu Nath from Banda in Uttar Pradesh cut his tongue off with a knife and laid it at the feet of a statue of the goddess Durga during Navratri, a nine-day Hindu festival that symbolises the victory of good over evil. Nath had told fellow festival-goers about the promise several days earlier, but no one had taken him seriously, clearly underestimating his deep reverence for the goddess.

Taking the Bible too literally can have bloody consequences. A Filipino man cut off his penis with a machete because he thought it was leading him to sin. The Christian convert from Bacolod City had no regrets about maiming himself, and his sinful penis was not found. Roland Magsipoc turned to the Bible after his wife left him three years ago and his family believe he was influenced by the book of Matthew 18:8, which states that a limb should be cut off if it causes a person to sin.

THINGS IN HUMANS THAT SHOULDN'T BE THERE

An Indian doctor removed a 4-inch leech that had spent three days inside a schoolboy's nostril. Ten-year-old Akhil said that the leech, which may have crept into his nose while he was drinking water from a tap, made him feel dizzy and caused his nose to bleed. Dr Sukhdev Singh of the Chandigarh General Hospital had

WEIRD

bone of contention

Asha, a six-year-old girl in India, was taken to New Delhi hospital after local doctors failed to find the cause of her chest pains. Initially x-rays suggested a tumour, but when they operated doctors were surprised to find that there was a fully formed jaw in her chest. It had been growing there since she was born, and had well-developed teeth, a tongue and part of an upper larynx.

never seen a leech up a patient's nostril during his fifteen-year career, but nevertheless, he knew what to do. When Akhil splashed water on his face, the leech appeared and Singh pulled it out with a pair of forceps.

Doctors in Dimitrovgrad in the Ulyanovsk region of Russia found a worm living under the skin of an elderly man. They removed the unwanted resident, known as Dirofilaria, from near the man's left eyelid. A similar case in the same area involved a woman who had lived for a year with a 2-inch worm under the skin of her forehead.

Doctors in Jodhpur, India, removed two 7-centimetre horns growing out of a woman's head. Doctors said that although the woman's grandfather, father and sister had developed similar horns, the deformity was not hereditary.

A couple of students at Bacau University, Romania, were both suffering with cold symptoms, but in neither case was a virus to blame. The first student, named as Maria P., went to her doctor with a headache. She was informed that a cockroach had managed to get into her inner ear where, fortunately for her, it had died. Another student named as Ana N. had a runny nose, but no other cold symptoms, and when she blew her nose, out came a cockroach. Following these two incidents students at the residence where these intrusive cockroaches were rife started sleeping with ear and nose plugs.

The events in this story actually occurred four years ago, but the report was only recently released in a medical journal, *The Archives of Internal Medicine*. Two patients in a Missouri, USA, hospital who were in comas were found to have maggots growing in their nostrils, coming from flies which had originally infested dead mice in the canteen area of the hospital. The maggots were described as 'ghastly but harmless' by one of the hospital's doctors.

In the Russian city of Ulyanovsk a women consulted her doctor about a large lump that had appeared on her leg. The doctor inspected the lump and decided that it was in no way malignant. He then made an incision in the woman's leg, and out crawled an 8-centimetre-long worm. Apparently it was a parasite that typically lives in dogs, not commonly known to take up residence in humans.

TATTOO TALES

A disturbing tattoo trend has emerged this year in Russia. Naked and chained politicians have replaced naked women as Russian prisoners' favourite tattoo subjects, according to a piece of research carried out by Danzig Baldaïev. This would suggest, perhaps, that politics has become more important to prisoners than sex. Could this be true? One of the most popular tattoos is of a drunken Mikhail Gorbachev with 'Let's fight against the vodka' written underneath.

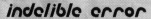

indelible error

Mark Brewer, an avid Arsenal fan, had the crest of that football club tattooed on his arm, blissfully unaware that in two short weeks his beloved club would unveil a brand new crest. Mr Brewer, from Hampshire, also named three of his children after Arsenal players, shortly after which all three players were transferred to other clubs. In his most recent show of support he paid £50 to have the club's cannon crest tattooed on his left arm. On the new crest the cannon points in the opposite direction.

Gordon Roy of Wishaw, Scotland, could think of no better way to pay tribute to a friend who had died in a road accident than to have the entire lyrics to rock band Led Zeppelin's classic song 'Stairway To Heaven' tattooed on his back. Tattooist Dave McGowan had never had a request like it. Gordon did it because he and his friend both loved the song so much.

IMPALEMENTS

In Knoxville, in the US state of Tennessee, a fifty-year-old construction worker got the point – literally – about safety regulations when he was impaled from above by a 3-foot-long, 3-inch-thick metal rod that fell from a bridge. It went point-first through his skull and neck, continued vertically down his trunk, and ended up

fat chance

Being obese can kill you, but for 21-stone Stuart Crane of Carmarthen, Wales, it saved his life. Stuart's car careered off the road and into a field,

where a fence post plunged through the car door, into the right side of Stuart's ample 46-inch belly and out the other side. The thirty-two-year-old lost four ribs, suffered a collapsed lung and a torn bowel, and had to have 900 stitches, but surgeons told him his massive gut had protected his vital organs. Stuart's reaction when the car skidded to a standstill and he saw that the 2-foot 4-inch post had punctured his paunch was to phone his sister on his mobile phone and tell her he had a bit of a splinter in him. Numb with shock, he then dialled 999, was rushed to hospital and underwent three hours of surgery to remove the post. Stuart kept the stake as a souvenir and vowed never to go on a diet that might risk him losing his lucky belly.

completely embedded in his body. He was semi-conscious at the scene but talkative later in the hospital. The man had not been wearing the obligatory hard hat.

COLESLAW WRESTLING INCIDENT

In Samsala, Florida, USA, there is an annual Bike Week celebration in which up to 500,000 bikers from all over the nation put on their best leather and denim to take part. As part of the festivities, one of the town's hostelries, Sopotnick's Cabbage Patch bar, sponsors a coleslaw wrestling match each year, in which women wrestlers grapple in a pit of cabbage and oil for the pleasure of the leering bikers. The bizarre accident occurred when a parachutist, hired to parachute in on the festival, was blown off course by high winds and cannoned into a waitress carrying a tray of drinks right by the coleslaw pit. The victim, Sherri Lee, thirty-seven, suffered head and facial injuries and was taken to hospital, where she was reported to be in a serious but stable condition. The skydiver, who said he never saw the woman, was uninjured. And those poor bikers had their grapple 'n' grope-fest delayed by a whole 15 minutes.

STUCK

In Vienna, a man fleeing muggers escaped into a portable public toilet and locked himself in. Irritated, the muggers rolled the toilet over with the door face down and left the man. He remained there for three long, hot days before being rescued, enduring temperatures of over 30°C.

Theresa Moorer of Marbury, Alabama, USA, was carried over 20 miles in a 90,000-pound garbage compactor to a landfill site where she narrowly avoided meeting her death. She had been partying a bit too hard in the town of Valley, and after leaving the party had crawled on to a mattress she saw inside an open rubbish

ODD

white-buttock ride

Clearly portable toilets are dangerous places. In Morro Bay, California, USA, a chain gang from a local prison was working at the roadside, and provided with a Port-a-Potty for convenience. One of the convicts was relieving himself when the Port-a-Potty truck hooked it up and drove it away. The terrified inmate was taken on a white-knuckle ride which stopped only when a pedestrian spotted the tilting Port-a-Potty with a clearly distressed man trying to get out of it. The onlooker called the police, who freed the prisoner then took him back to jail.

bin and fallen asleep. Hours later she awoke when a landfill worker caught sight of her leg poking out of a pile of furniture and thought there was a corpse in the trash. Theresa was disoriented but otherwise unhurt, police said, and could not remember why she'd crawled on to the mattress in the first place. The police also found 'drugs paraphernalia' in her purse, but did not file charges since her day had already been pretty bad.

Kevin Funchess, forty-one, popped out to get some fried chicken in his home town of Houston, Texas, USA, and fell through a manhole into a storm drain. Firmly wedged about 3 metres below the surface of the road, Kevin was unable to twist round and get his mobile phone out of his backpack. Shouting for help didn't work either and poor Kevin spent three whole days stuck there, unable to move and hearing his phone ring repeatedly as family members tried to contact him. Eventually, through lack of food and water, Kevin lost enough weight to be able to twist round and reach that precious mobile phone to call emergency services. He was finally rescued and was not too much the worse for wear. He said he had spent most of his time sleeping and praying.

Even if you're a fully paid-up, card-carrying sado-masochist, there comes a point when enough's enough. An Italian man appeared naked and hand-cuffed on a Rotterdam balcony after escaping from a cage where he'd been imprisoned for several days by his 'masters' (later arrested by police). The man had been locked up when a sex party got out of control, and, having been kicked and beaten for a few days, then found that he stopped enjoying his imprisonment. He slipped from the second-floor flat's balcony and landed on a lower one, by this time in a state of panic.

help, i'm stupid

A terrified, panic-stricken call from an inner-city phone box in New Zealand led police to the rescue of a man who was, he said, stuck inside, totally unable to get out. The clever, resourceful policemen had him out of there in just seconds – the man had been pulling the door instead of pushing.

Fifty-year-old Floyd Goodman was working for the Golden Peanut Company in Suffolk, Virginia, USA, when he had a little accident. He fell off a catwalk in the storage warehouse and plunged into 12 feet of peanuts. His co-workers immediately feared the worst, since five other similar incidents had all ended in death. Luckily, however, Goodman had the presence of mind to pull his dust mask over his face and cup his hands over it, preventing him from inhaling the potentially fatal dust and allowing him a little space to breathe. He lay there for about an hour and a quarter before firemen could get to him. He was taken to hospital with only minor injuries.

IT'S CRUNCH TIME!

Workers at a South Carolina, USA, car firm were lucky to escape unhurt when a huge slab of ice crashed through their roof. The slab sliced through the building's roof 'like through a piece of paper' according to the fire captain of the town of West Ashley, and demolished a car. Aviation officials said that there was no air traffic overhead at the time, so the best guess is that the slab was from the edge of a passing meteor.

The Utah, USA, desert town of Rockville really lived up to its name when a giant boulder broke clear from a hillside above the town. The 16-foot-wide boulder broke off during the night and rolled straight into the home of Jack Burns as he slept. Jack's bedroom and bathroom were destroyed, but more disturbingly the boulder came within 2 feet of his head. Jack said that although he was woken by the noise of breaking glass he didn't have time to jump out of bed. And he didn't realise what a near miss he'd had until day broke and he saw for himself the giant rock embedded in his home.

FLYING MANHOLE COVERS

Manhole covers shooting up into the air seems to be on the increase. They really should glue them down or something.

During the sweltering heat of summer, the American capital, Washington DC, had to deal with a case of flying manhole covers. In the upmarket shopping district of Georgetown the chunky metal discs were spotted shooting vertically upwards several feet into the air, apparently due to pressure caused by subterranean fires. Fortunately, nobody was hurt, but the phenomenon occurred frequently enough for a restaurant in the Georgetown area to create a cocktail called 'the Exploding Manhole Cover'.

A spectacular manhole son et lumière took place in the eastern Chinese city of Chuzhou, where the sewers were beset by a series of deafening explosions that blew manhole covers several feet into the air, followed by huge columns of fire. The display continued for a good five hours before the fire service managed to get things under control. It is thought that the explosions were caused by petrol leaking into the sewers from a service station.

flying man

Flying manhole covers struck again, this time in the northern Mexican city of Monterrey, with one unnamed individual having a particularly huge slice of bad luck. An underground explosion of methane gas blew out a manhole cover on which our man happened to be standing. He shot 25 feet into the air, hitting live electrical wires that gave him second-degree burns, before falling back down and on to the roof of a passing bus, sustaining fractures to an arm and hip on impact.

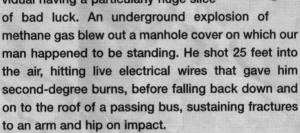

In New York City a manhole cover shot up beneath a school bus in Harlem, causing it to crash into two parked cars. That very same week a manhole cover in Manhattan blew beneath a taxi, bursting through the floor of the car.

GLUE

It's very sticky. Remember that. Some people forget …

A driver in Italy was stuck to the road when the lorry in front of him shed its load of construction glue. The lorry crashed into a tree on the Bressana bridge between Milan and Pavia, and gallons of extra-strong glue flooded the tarmac, bringing the car behind to a sticky halt. In a move worthy of a cartoon gag, the driver got out to see what had happened and he immediately became stuck to the road. He had his mobile phone with him, though, and called for help. Rescue workers eventually dissolved the glue and everyone came unstuck.

A student at the University of Toledo, Ohio, USA, needed surgery when a friend glued his eyelid shut as a joke. Doctors had to remove most of his eyelashes when they used a scalpel to prise open Aaron Laser's eyelid eight days after the incident. Laser was targeted while, visiting friends, he fell asleep on a sofa.

A British man ended up in hospital after gluing his mobile phone to his hand. Terry Chivers, from Wiltshire, managed to drive himself to the accident and emergency unit of the hospital with the phone still attached to his hand, after he'd made a bit of a mess of trying to repair the handset.

superglue surgery ODD

A Turkish bus driver in Antalya was attacked by a gang of knife-wielding youths. They stole money and his mobile phone, and also sliced off part of his ear for good measure. Recep Yavrucu wasn't too keen on going to hospital, though, because he had a terrible fear of doctors and needles and all that sort of thing. So instead he bought a tube of superglue and glued the ear part back on. He said afterwards that he always treated his own wounds.

WHOOPS!

Crucial decisions need to be made correctly. These weren't. The results stand out a mile.

The world's biggest sundial was finally completed in Gosport, Hampshire – and it is in the shade of a fifteen-storey block of flats. In addition, the Millennium Timespace, as the sundial is called, was to have been completed for the Millennium but arrived eighteen months late.

The Mersey Tunnel, a famous landmark in Liverpool, takes a lot of traffic, including, of course, buses. Odd, then, that when Arriva North West spent £7 million on a new fleet of buses in Merseyside they turned out to be too big to go through the tunnel. The mistake was discovered when the first bus went out on the route and the driver had to take his passengers on an 8-mile detour because of the 1.5-inch discrepancy.

The world's biggest advertising billboard, measuring a whopping 900 by 135 yards, was built on the banks of the Yangtze river in Chongqing, China, and even got a mention in the *Guinness Book of Records*. Well, it may have been big, but hardly anyone ever saw it because it was enveloped in fog for almost the entire year. In three years the giant site failed to attract one single advertisement and had to be scrapped.

A MISTAKE ANYONE COULD MAKE

A German woman from Kiel drove away in the wrong car after arranging to borrow her sister's car. The car she drove off in was a Mazda, and her sister's car was a white Volkswagen, but of course they were practically impossible to tell apart because the Mazda, parked next to the Volkswagen, was white too. Unfortunately, the VW keys not only opened the door of the Mazda

right fire, wrong place

A Romanian man set fire to himself to protest at having to wait for financial support from the authorities. Unfortunately for him the impact of his protest was lost as he did it outside the wrong building. He should have been setting light to himself outside the Town Hall, but his act of self-immolation took place outside the County Hall. He survived and promised to be more careful in future about getting his location right.

WEIRD

going off half-cock STUPID

In a desperately unfortunate accident in Peru, a policeman shot off his partner's penis. Officers Siloe Espinoza and Baiver Ruelas were changing into their uniforms at Lima police station when Espinoza pulled his revolver out of its holster to see if it was loaded. He didn't check where it was pointing though and accidentally pulled the trigger.

but also worked in the ignition, so the woman had the car all day before noticing, when she got into it again to return it to her sister, that she hadn't got the right one. She called the police to explain and was not charged with theft (just with the inability to tell the difference between a Mazda and a VW).

The city of Birmingham was more than a little short-sighted when its council evicted a blind tenant from his flat and changed the locks while he was out, trapping his guide dog inside. The council had sent him a written notice, but not in Braille.

All Susan Robertson of Fife, Scotland, wanted was to give her husband a special birthday treat in the form of a nice trifle. Realising she'd run out of sherry, she hunted around in the drinks cabinet for a good alternative and came up with an unmarked bottle of Scotch. Little did she know, as she poured copious amounts of the bottle's contents into the trifle, that it was an extremely rare millennium whisky specially produced by the Macallan distillery and worth £2,000. David Robertson took it all with good grace, pronouncing it to be the best trifle he'd ever tasted.

Ermes Zamperla, a human cannonball by trade, was injured after overshooting his target at a fair in Florida, USA. He landed on his feet after missing his inflatable cushion by about 8 metres, but then crashed head first into a temporary fibreglass fence. He was admitted to Tampa General Hospital with broken bones and a head injury.

A couple were out duck shooting on Lake Colangulac, in Australia's Victoria state. The twenty-five-year-old woman and her twenty-nine-year-old man were in an aluminium punt, and when the woman reached over the side to retrieve a duck she had just shot, she fell in, still holding her gun. Seeing that her waders would fill with water and drag her under, her partner grabbed her quickly, causing her to spin round suddenly. As she turned, her gun went off, a bullet hitting and killing him instantly.

A surgeon at Rhode Island Hospital in Providence, Rhode Island, USA operated on the wrong side of a man's head because the patient's brain scan was placed backwards on the viewing box. The man, who was suffering from bleeding on the brain, did not suffer any long-term damage.

When Edoardo Q's wife died in 1988 he vowed to visit and pray at her tomb every single day. Imagine his surprise when he found that for the last eleven years he had been praying at the wrong tomb. Under the tombstone bearing her picture and name was a man; his wife's body was somewhere else in the graveyard, having been the subject of a general reallocation of tombs. Edoardo, from Cesano Maderno in northern Italy, is demanding compensation.

With military precision, a crack team of Royal Artillery soldiers arrived at a primary school fete in Colchester, Essex, set up an assault course and gave a display of their soldierly skills. Only it was the wrong school.

The world's first fully automated car park was designed to take a shopper's car, park it and later return it, all at the touch of a button. But the software of the system, operating in Zurich, Switzerland, crashed, leaving everyone who had entrusted their car to it stranded. Many of the car owners had to be put up in hotels overnight by the city council.

A Polish animal rights group staged a protest at a farm in Opole regarding a field full of cattle being kept in simply atrocious conditions during the bitter Polish winter. It turned out, however, that the cattle were a Canadian breed that thrives in cold conditions.

it seemed like a good idea at the time

A Norwegian man wanted to buy some beer from his local town of Krager, south-west of Oslo. However, he thought that rather than going round by road, he would take a shortcut and swim there (only about a mile along the coast). Tying his shoes round his neck and with his credit card gripped between his clenched teeth, the thirty-five-year-old struck out along the Skagerrak coast, and was pulled off course by strong currents. Two hours later he was still out there, and witnesses called the police, who had to send a boat out to rescue him.

In 2002, Queen Elizabeth's Golden Jubilee year, there was more than a little money to be made selling flags to wave during the celebrations. So, as you can imagine, there were a few red faces when a customer at Langley's toy shop in Norwich, noticed that the Union flag he was buying had 'Made in Germany' on the label. The flags were made by German company Riethmuller, one of the world's leading suppliers of party hats, flags and balloons. It transpires that there are no British companies producing the little paper flags.

A brother and sister from Florida, USA, went to a great deal of trouble to fulfil their mother's last request. Donna and Gary Bellos travelled the world to

come out, we've got someone else covered

Paul Goldsmythe was watching a late night film on TV at his home in Christchurch, New Zealand, when the phone rang. It was the police and their message was unsettlingly clear: your house is surrounded – come out with no weapons and your hands in the air or you'll be shot. Terrified, Paul did as he was told and walked slowly out in front of his house and down the driveway, arms in the air – to find the street deserted. Meanwhile the police, surrounding a house a kilometre away, realised they'd dialled the wrong number. Police spokeswoman Maggie Leask said police obtained Mr Goldsmythe's phone number from a group confronted about a shooting incident earlier in the night.

visit the places where their late mother had enjoyed some of her most precious moments, scattering some of her cremated ashes at each spot. It was a beautiful request, sensitively and conscientiously executed. The only problem was that they later discovered that the ashes they had scattered were not those of their mother since they had been given the wrong urn. You can be sure that Donna and Gary are now suing the ass off the E. Earl Smith & Son funeral home.

NO OFFENCE INTENDED

Of course it wasn't a serious offer, but the Mayor himself took offence, when a Cincinnati, USA, radio station ran a competition offering a free, yes free, coffin to the city's hundredth shooting victim. The aim of the spoof was to open up the debate on gun crime – but it clearly backfired.

The editor of the *Concord Monitor*, a newspaper in New Hampshire, USA, was forced to apologise for his decision to run a cartoon featuring New York's World Trade Center twin towers being hit by a plane. In the satirical cartoon, the plane was labelled 'Bush Budget', while the towers were called 'Social Security'. A good point, perhaps, but it could have been made with just a little more sensitivity.

When a barrister, a Mr Cartmel, announced the Queen Mother's death to a packed courtroom in Newcastle there were gasps from around the court, and two female jurors burst into tears as he paid a short tribute to her. Then the recorder, David Wakeman, also stood up to talk of the sad loss to the nation. It was only when Mr Cartmel got home and watched the TV news that he realised that what he had been told was nothing more than a rumour, and as a barrister he really ought to have got his facts right. Mr Cartmel apologised profusely to the court the following day. At the time of writing, Her Majesty the Queen Mother was very much alive.

The Red Mist

OVERREACTING

What's in a name? Well, apparently rather a lot: in the Philippines, Randy Cruz stabbed his neighbour, Rogelio Lopez, to death during a bitter argument about which of their surnames was the better.

Thirty-nine-year-old Lee Barter was sentenced in Portsmouth for stabbing a friend twice during a game of Trivial Pursuit in which his mate committed the unforgivable crime of cheating by adding extra cheeses to his counter.

A fifty-seven-year-old man went into a restaurant in Temuco, Chile, ordered a slap-up meal and put away a bottle of wine before sneaking off without paying. His waiter was so incensed that after his shift, he tracked the man down to where he was sleeping rough in an abandoned house, and stabbed him to death.

Eighteen-year-old Rajender Singh, from northern India took some stick from his friends, who said he would be better off taking care of his father's bangle shop than joining the army to fight Pakistan in the event of a war. Rajender, unamused, got himself a box of 1-inch nails and drove them into his feet and hands. That showed them he was tough enough.

A woman from Yeovil, Somerset, felt obliged to sell her shiny new sports car after spotting a spider on the passenger seat one day. She now has to rely on friends to get to work each day.

In the Malaysian village of Sandakan a carpenter went berserk, killing two workmates and a woman and leaving another woman with multiple slash wounds on her body after friends teased him over being dumped by his girlfriend. He had proposed to her and been turned down, leaving him heartbroken and, it transpired, extremely dangerous.

Twenty-two-year-old Enrique Nunez, of Chicago, USA, went ballistic when four teenagers openly ridiculed his half-brother's haircut. Ismael Higuera had gone for the 'shaved-all-over-except-for-a-small-bit-at-the-back-that's-grown-into-a-long-ponytail' style, and when the four laughed at him in a fast food joint, he called Nunez and asked him to come armed. Enrique defended the hairstyle's honour by firing into the teenagers' car, hitting one in the leg and another in the foot.

At his shop in New Delhi, India, Sunder Singh was challenged by a rival pigeon fancier Rakesh Kumar, who said that his pigeons were of royal pedigree while Singh's were a cheap variety. So, as any enraged pigeon seller worth his salt would, he got his gun and began firing randomly in the street, resulting in four innocent passers-by being grazed by bullets and hospitalised.

A Chicago man was accused of killing his roommate during a row over a chicken dinner in which, it was claimed by prosecutors, the pair were arguing over who had the biggest portion. The victim was allegedly attacked with an ashtray, pliers, a

hurry up, honey

You'd think that doing the washing-up would win you a few brownie points rather than a stabbing. But no. In Billings, Montana, USA, Elizabeth Holt's boyfriend, James Demontiney, was washing the dishes too slowly. Unable to bear it any longer, Holt, who was in hurry to go out to visit her parents, ran at Demontiney with a 6-inch kitchen knife and plunged it into his back. It's not known whether this made him drop a plate, but she did at least call the emergency services and help to treat the wound until an ambulance arrived and took him to hospital.

hammer, a fire extinguisher, a dumbbell and a knife. The thirty-eight-year-old man was charged with first-degree murder.

RAGE:
SHOVELLING RAGE

In the German region of Thuringia police were called out on a couple of occasions when neighbourly niggles in winter turned into something much rougher. The problems arose from that Teutonic desire for order and cleanliness when it came to keeping drives free of snow. Both incidents happened when people were caught shovelling snow from their own doorsteps on to those of their neighbours, and in both cases evolved into full-blown fisticuffs. A sixty-six-year-old man was so badly beaten up that he was taken, concussed, to hospital, and a twenty-year-old man was swatted full in the face with a snow shovel.

CAB RAGE

A German woman was desperate to get a taxi home, and when she thought two men were trying to jump the queue at the taxi rank in Arnsberg, the red mist of cab rage overtook her. She bit one of the men so ferociously that she severed part of his thumb, and she scratched the hands of the other. Police officers managed to intervene before she did any more damage.

LIFT RAGE

Workers had to flee an office block in Montreal, Canada, due to an occurrence of lift rage. Two workers got into the lift at a high-rise office building, then got into an argument about whether the lift should go up or down. One of them attacked the other with pepper spray, which spread on to each floor that the lift stopped at, forcing a partial evacuation of the building and resulting in three workers being taken to hospital. Other workers panicked when they saw firefighters gathering around the building.

PAVEMENT RAGE

Jean Louis van Berkel of Hamilton, New Zealand, snapped when he found a car blocking his way on the pavement where he was walking with his toddler and dog. He kicked in all four doors of the car, then stamped on its boot, roof and bonnet, and told police when they arrived that he'd do whatever he had to do to be able to walk on 'the last free place on this earth'.

EXPRESS CHECKOUT RAGE

A woman in Lowell, Massachusetts, USA, attacked a fellow supermarket shopper for taking too many items to the express till. The thirty-eight-year-old woman began to argue with the other woman, who made the b-i-g mistake of taking thirteen items to the '12 items or fewer' till, then followed her outside and kicked and punched her.

RIDING TEST RAGE

The British Horse Society were obliged to change their testing procedure after several incidents of riding test rage, involving attacks on examiners. One attack was severe enough to merit calling out the police. The attacks mainly involved the parents of failed students, for whom failure after many thousands of pounds of tuition fees is not an option.

UNNECESSARY VIOLENCE

A lovable children's character was punched and kicked by an irate father in a Sesame Street theme park in Philadelphia, USA. Lee McPhatter was angered by the Cookie Monster's refusal to pose for a photograph with his little daughter, Mina, and he approached the blue, furry creature to remonstrate. Jennie McNelis, inside the suit, tried to move him aside, and he began shouting, poked his head inside the Cookie Monster's mouth, and, when she pushed him back, threw her to the ground and began punching and kicking. What the crowds of watching kids thought is anyone's guess.

A boy aged three attacked two women, leaving one with a fractured skull and another shaken and bruised having been hit by the boy's toy truck. Both women needed hospital treatment after the thirty-minute onslaught. It all took place in a pharmacy in Tauranga, New Zealand, when the toddler began kicking one woman in the shins. When she eventually bent

VIOLENCE

one in, all in

We know that Australia is a land where men are men (and sheep are nervous), but even by Outback standards this is pretty good. In the tiny Queensland town of Boulia (population 300), blazing hot weather was blamed for sparking a pub brawl that sucked in a third of the town's population. Yes, that's right, while temperatures hovered around 44°C, around a hundred people became involved in the fight, as families settled feuds, and a lot of beer was involved too. Boulia police force tried to break up the brawl but were forced to call for reinforcements from hundreds of kilometres away as fighters were observed going at it from one end of the block to the other. Only sixteen people were charged with public order offences, but the town's only pub was shut down for two days.

down to stop him, he beat her over the head with his truck. The second woman ran to her aid and the tiny terror turned on her, again lashing out with his truck. When they pleaded with the little boy's mother for help, she said she didn't know what to do about it. She told her son to apologise, but he hurled a mouthful of abuse and ran off. In an ironic twist, one of the women had recently come to live in the peaceful town of Tauranga from Palm Island, off Townsville in Queensland, a town listed by the *Guinness Book of Records* as the world's most violent place outside a combat zone. She had never once been hurt there.

At a high school in Texas, USA, a play was being performed as part of the school's annual Peace Week. The play, *Stop the Violence*, had only begun a few minutes earlier, when a fight broke out as one student assaulted another. Many of the crowd joined in and the police had to be called to restore order.

In the usually peaceful town of Terrace in the very peaceful Canadian province of British Columbia, a forty-year-old man smashed a cinema's soda fountain and cash register, as well as a plant in the lobby, because he was upset at the excessive violence in the film *Lord of the Rings*.

Treavor Harvey of Sarasota, Florida, USA, is president of a community group called Mad Dads, an anti-violence group, whose aim is to steer kids away from crime and violence. So we can understand that

third time lucky?

Five years ago an Ethiopian man from the Oromo region was convicted of trying to kill his own brother by throwing an explosive device at him. He failed, and was jailed for five years. His time inside clearly had no effect and as soon as he was released from jail he struck again. This time he pushed his wife off a cliff, only to watch her land safely in a haystack 140 feet below.

when he was coaching his son's football team he complained to the referee that the game was getting too rough. However, he did his cause no favours when he went ahead and punched the ref, getting himself arrested for assault in the process.

Pillars of the Community

POLITICS ...

It seemed to Mabel Briscoe that the state of Maryland was not demanding enough ID from its voters. To prove her point, she registered her Jack Russell terrier on the electoral roll as Holly Briscoe. Holly was soon called up for jury service, while eighty-two-year-old Mabel was charged with voter fraud by the state of Maryland.

In St Louis, USA, councillors were quite clear that if Irene Smith were to leave the council chamber during a filibuster speech she would lose the floor – even if it was for an urgent toilet visit. So her aides concealed her modesty behind sheets and she relieved herself into a handy receptacle, it was alleged when she was charged with urinating into a wastebasket.

You can just imagine them facing each other over a card table in a Wild West saloon. Noel Perran moves his hand to the deck of cards in front of him and draws a card. It is the seven of hearts. Edward Libby pulls the deck over, pulls a card out and flips it nonchalantly on to the table. Ten of clubs. He wins the election for Colorado local council. And apart from the Wild West stuff, that's how it really happened. They both polled forty-seven votes and agreed to settle it by drawing cards.

... AND POLITICIANS

Bribery is obviously far too strong a word for Australian MP John Elferink's actions, but fellow Aussie politicians weren't too happy with his way of winning voters' affections. Elferink had handed out good-will severed kangaroo tails as he canvassed his mainly Aboriginal constituents.

Not a politician yet, but surely a glittering career awaits: Lal Bihari's method of attracting voters' interest in Uttar Pradesh, India, was to pretend to be a

CANDID

at last, the truth

The Spanish Prime Minister gave a speech to the European Parliament and sat down to a rousing round of applause. Believing his microphone to be switched off, José Maria Aznar then gave his own verdict on the speech: 'What nonsense I have just come out with,' a comment that was clearly heard by those around him.

corpse that suddenly comes alive. His supporters would carry him around in a coffin, come to a halt and Lal would throw off the cloth that covered him and scream that he was alive. His main political point was that inaccurate local records listed 3,000 people as being dead who, in fact, weren't.

An American politician was jailed for his third drunk driving conviction, but pledged to go on representing his constituents from behind bars. Kevin Ryan, forty-nine, a state representative in Connecticut was sentenced to 120 days in jail, and had been a staunch supporter of moves to tighten drink-driving laws.

Bob Hunter, the Liberal party candidate for a Toronto City Council seat, was forced to go back on his word: during his election campaign it was revealed that thirteen years earlier he had written a book giving an account of a round-the-world trip that included sex sessions with underage girls in Thailand. According to the book's blurb all the stories were true, but Hunter now insisted that the underage sex bit was a 'middle-aged man's fantasy to make a satirical point about ... the decadence of Western culture'. He lost the election but still got 36 per cent of the vote.

There was definitely something unusual about the Humanist Party candidate for Central Santiago during Chile's general election: he was dead. No more. Gone to meet his maker. Raul Veloso, whose name was mistakenly included on the ballot papers, still managed to poll over a thousand votes though. The main reason for Veloso's posthumous popularity seems to be the mode of his death which appealed to the people so much that they voted for his memory. Raul, an ex-plumber, snuffed it during sex, after having taken a cocktail of drugs and alcohol.

RELIGION ...

Israel's El Al airline was faced with a request that really tested their PR skills. Ultra-orthodox Jews of priestly heritage asked to be allowed to travel inside body bags, to avoid becoming ritually unclean when flying over a Jewish cemetery (a recent ruling by prominent ultra-orthodox rabbi Yosef Shalom Elyashiv had extended the ban on Jews descended from biblical priests from entering cemeteries to include overflights). The request was eventually rejected by the airline.

 A fast-spreading sect named Lightning from the East has been winning large numbers of converts

take me, lord

Driving one evening with her husband, an American woman was seized by religious fervour as she caught sight of Jesus and his twelve disciples at the roadside. Convinced it was the Second Coming, she leapt out of the car's sunroof and, tragically, met her death on the road. Her vision was, in fact, one Ernie Jenkins on his way to a fancy dress party, dressed as Jesus, complete with twelve helium-filled sex dolls as his followers.

to its unorthodox tenets in China. Its followers believe that Jesus has returned to earth as a plain-looking, thirty-year-old Chinese woman (who conveniently lives in hiding and has never been photographed). They credit her with composing a third testament to the Bible, writing enough hymns to fill ten CDs and teaching that Christians who join her will ascend to heaven in the coming apocalypse.

The only two remaining Jewish residents of Kabul, Afghanistan, Isaac Levy, fifty-seven, and Zebolan Simonto, forty-one, were still locked in a bitter dispute after three years. Described as a 'relentless, petty feud', their grievance began when both claimed ownership of a handwritten edition of the Torah. Simonto eventually succeeded in having Levy imprisoned as an Israeli spy, which prompted Levy to get

Simonto imprisoned, accusing him of trying to convert Muslims to Christianity. Both men run their own synagogue, neither of which has any congregants for obvious reasons.

...AND PRIESTS

The Father Superior of Pupping Monastery in northern Austria introduced a novel way of ensuring that his monks get to prayers on time. He bought a firemen's pole from a local shop, visited Linz fire brigade for installation advice, then ran the pole from the second floor sleeping quarters to the ground floor. Father Wenigwieser feels that plunging 7 metres in two seconds is a wonderful way to start the day, and there's a special cushioned base so that the older or stouter brothers land safely. And most importantly, since the pole was installed no one has been late for prayers – even though not one of the monastery's nuns has dared to use it.

faith versus reality

ODD

A preacher in the Congo proclaimed to his followers that he could walk on water like Jesus, and hundreds watched in horror as he made his attempt on the fast-flowing River Kwipu and was instantly swept away to his death. His body was recovered by his followers, and we can only hope that his soul has ascended to heaven.

An Italian priest prevented a marriage ceremony from taking place because he felt that the bride was showing too much of her bosom. Don Pier Giuseppe Gaude would not allow the bride to enter the Santa Rita parish in Turin and told the congregation to 'go in peace'. The bride, known only as Isabella, later married her fiancé in a civil ceremony.

A Catholic priest told believers that the end of the world was nigh then stole their belongings. Father Fernando Vallejo led around two hundred people on to a farm near Florencia, Colombia, and told them to wait there for the end of the world before making off with the money and personal possessions that they had given him on being told that property was an obstacle to salvation.

After a drinking binge, Father Boris, priest in the Bulgarian village of Bistriza, decided to shoot his pistol in the air, but missed and shot himself in the leg. Police subsequently charged him with illegal gun possession.

OH, AND JUDGES

In the USA, Pittsburgh Common Pleas judge H. Patrick McFalls Jr had been a very naughty boy indeed, and the Pennsylvania Judicial Conduct Board was having difficulty in deciding how to deal with allegations about his behaviour. They included: creating a disturbance at an airport ticket counter; 'giving' his $60,000 car to a young man then, forgetting having done so, reporting the car stolen; being arrested for creating a disturbance with a cab driver about the fare while visiting Miami Beach; removing his trousers at a restaurant; being arrested at a theatre for becoming boisterous during a movie; and allowing his trousers to fall down several times while having an animated conversation in the street. Still, he's probably a very good judge. And that's what counts.

BOTCHED OPERATIONS

Surgeons and dentists have such huge workloads and get so tired that they're bound to make a teeny little mistake now and again ...

where's that retractor gone?

After Donald Church had surgery in Seattle, USA, to remove a tumour, his appendix and part of his intestine, the pain just never went away. All part of the healing process, he was confidently told at a thirty-day check-up. That healing process seemed, weirdly, to be setting off airport metal detectors, as well as stopping Mr Church's bowels from working properly. Not to mention the searing pain. A visit to his own doctor led to a CAT scan which revealed the awful truth: doctors had stitched a 13-inch metal retractor, used to hold the edges of surgical incisions open, inside him during the operation, a rare mistake, for which the University of Seattle Medical Centre agreed to pay Church $97,000. Church had the retractor removed at a different hospital.

A Swedish woman from Gothenburg had been suffering from sinus problems for a couple of years, and funnily enough, the problems seemed to have started around the time she had had a spot of dental treatment. The problem eventually got to the point where her left nostril was completely blocked. Shortly afterwards she felt something tickling the back of her throat. She reached in and pulled out a cotton swab that the dentist had left behind. Medical authorities told the dentist to be more careful in future.

Annick Sibille of Woippy, France, endured twenty-four years of stomach pains which doctors dismissed as purely psychosomatic. Well, they know best, don't they? But during an operation on a blood vessel near her spleen it turned out that there was a cotton pad inside her, left there by surgeons

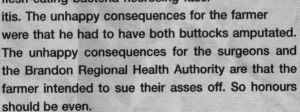

a slice of bad luck

A farmer in Manitoba, Canada, underwent colon surgery and during the operation contracted the dreaded flesh-eating bacteria necrosing fasciitis. The unhappy consequences for the farmer were that he had to have both buttocks amputated. The unhappy consequences for the surgeons and the Brandon Regional Health Authority are that the farmer intended to sue their asses off. So honours should be even.

during an operation back in 1977. Not surprisingly, Annick decided to sue.

This story isn't about bad medics, but bad beauticians. A woman in Kansas City, USA, went into her beauty salon to have her acrylic nails removed and a new set put on. Reba Burgess sat while the nail technician started to take off the old nails. According to Ms Burgess, the technician filed, then drilled, then picked, then drilled, then filed and soaked, and the nails didn't come off. Whenever Ms Burgess asked when they would be finished, the technician replied that it would be just a little longer. Four hours later Ms Burgess's hands were bleeding, and, as it turned out, her bones had become infected. The result was that Ms Burgess had to have part of her index finger amputated. The salon settled out of court.

HAVING OBJECTS REMOVED FROM YOU

A thirty-three-year-old man was taken to the Via Christi Medical Center in Wichita, Kansas, USA, with a coat hanger stuck in his throat. The perfectly reasonable and logical explanation for this was that he'd been at a party, and he was told that someone (ah, that mysterious 'someone') had slipped a little ballon into his drink and he'd accidentally swallowed it. He then found out from 'someone' that this little balloon contained cocaine, a drug that he didn't want floating around in his system, oh no. So he immediately tried to

WEIRD

pls txt me now

How times change. In London, a hospital consultant came forward with the helpful information that there was a new problem in casualty when it came to male auto-erotic injuries. Whereas before the standard case had been a vacuum attachment stuck on the male member, the prevailing problem was now reported to be vibrating mobile phones stuck in the rectum.

hook it out with a coat hanger. Surgeons at the hospital sorted the man out, recovering both coat hanger and the little cocaine-filled balloon, but police were also on hand to charge him with drug possession.

ALTERNATIVE THERAPIES

Many people look down their noses at unorthodox treatments and therapies. But they can help, as these stories show.

A primary school in Wiltshire has turned itself from a failing school, according to its last government report, full of undisciplined, unruly, unteachable kids, into a successful one in just eighteen months. How? By the magical power of T'ai Chi. Every morning all fifty-six pupils and five staff are led through a ten-minute session in the school playground by one of the teachers, and the result is calm, focused children and a flourishing school.

Just to prove that no group of people is too hard or tough to resist the New Age, the macho miners of the Coppabella Mine in northern Queensland, Australia have been given free yoga clases by the owners, Macarthur Coal. Fatigue-related accidents have been a problem, apparently, and the aim is that the yoga will help workers to become more alert and also more flexible.

In Edinburgh, Scotland, traffic wardens are subject to abuse on the streets. Nothing unusual in that, except that they are now being offered shamanic meditation sessions, including shamanic drumming, to help to relieve the stress.

PROCEDURES YOU CAN LIVE WITHOUT

Prosperous South Koreans have become obsessive about the need for their children to reach a high standard in English, and it is now widely believed that snipping the tissue along the underside of the tongue will make it possible for children to pronounce the English 'r' and 'l' sounds. So off those kids go to outpatients to have a swift snip, or frenectomy, as it is called, despite the fact that many authorities believe that tongue shape has nothing top do with pronunciation difficulties: it's all cultural, they say. By the way, this is not a tongue-in-cheek report.

A Californian businessman is making a huge contribution to the welfare of the human race (not!) and raking in thousands of dollars from sad, vain men who live in fear of baldness. Operating under the name 'Hairogenics Inc.', Mike Blaylock thinks it is only a matter of time before scientists can make new hair from the strands of old ones. So customers pay him – $50 for the initial collection and an annual storage fee of $10 – to store strands of their hair in a climate-controlled cellar below a hair salon in Portland, Oregon. At the time of writing, despite the fact that the service was not officially open, nearly 200 men had signed up, not all of them bald. One such customer said, 'It's a precaution. Even if I don't go bald, maybe when I get old, there might be a way for me to get my young hair back.'

STRANGE CONDITIONS

Some people just can't be content to catch a cold every now and then. They've got to have something weird …

Fifteen-year-old Welsh schoolgirl, Michelle Jessett, has suffered agony every time she cries ever since an accident affected her by making her weep acid tears. Her bizarre condition apparently began when a lorry carrying chemicals burst into flames and sent a toxic cloud across the countryside. Michelle was on a school bus which passed the accident scene with open windows, unaware of the cloud of hydrochloric acid. Now whenever she cries her face is seared by acid, and her skin erupts in blisters. Doctors were baffled both as to cause and treatment.

James Wannerton has a rare condition known as synaesthesia. In his case it makes him taste a particular flavour when certain words are spoken. For example when he hears the word 'motorcycle' he can taste Rice Krispies; and his mouth fills with the flavour of Garibaldi biscuits whenever he hears the word 'key'. As a child he thought it was normal when, for example, reciting the Lord's Prayer, to taste bacon when he came to the word 'trespass'. And his love life has been influenced by his condition – he's chosen and finished with girlfriends because of the name-flavour association. The name Tracy tastes of flaky pastry to James; fortunately he's now found a girl whose name provokes no taste reaction – Janette.

A Texas man shot his girlfriend because he thought she was about to say 'New Jersey'. Thomas Ray Mitchell, fifty-four, gets incredibly angry when he hears certain phrases. Relatives testified that Thomas Ray curses and bangs on walls when he hears the words 'Snickers', 'Mars', 'Wisconsin' and, as we know, 'New Jersey'. He had spent some short periods in mental facilities since 1985, but had never harmed anyone saying those deadly words, until now. When he was arrested for the shooting, he admitted that he thought Barbara Jenkins was about to say 'New Jersey', but in the trial he did not claim insanity as a defence. While his relatives testified, Thomas Ray had to hold his ears closed with his fingers. The jury took less than two hours to convict him of aggravated assault with a deadly weapon.

women can be so fickle

When the first man in Romania to have a sex change operation decided it was no good being a woman and asked to be changed back again, he was told by doctors that the surgery he/she had undergone was irreversible. Sorina Ratiu, who was operated on in 1996, said she wanted to revert back to being a man because she couldn't have sex since her sexual organs did not function properly and also because her boyfriend left her when he discovered she had previously been a man. Sorina's boyfriend may also have noticed that she had not lost her manly body hair.

MAKE UP YOUR MIND ...

The man who received the world's first hand transplant, in 1998, a New Zealander by the name of Clint Hallam wasn't happy with his new hand and later had it removed. Now, however, he's told surgeons that he's changed his mind again and wants another hand.

Keep It In the Family

PARENTING

It's so hard to be a good parent. Not so hard to be a weird one though …

It was a bad month to be a kid in Florida when two spookily similar incidents occurred independently of each other within a three-week period.

WEIRD

that's my boy

A man from Cleveland, USA, was charged with felonious assault for trying to mould his five-month-old son's head to make it look more like his own. Joshua Brissett, nineteen, pleaded not guilty to the head-moulding attempts on his son, Roosevelt Worsham. The baby's mother, Shiara Worsham, was charged with child endangering, because she had seen Brissett using his hands to try to shape the infant's head and had waited three days before taking him to hospital after he had become ill.

First, police in Casselberry charged a twenty-nine-year-old woman with leaving her two children, twelve and eight, locked inside her storage locker all day while she was at work, with no plumbing or ventilation and with temperatures climbing above 30°C. Her response was to argue that, at 12 feet by 20, it was one of the larger lockers on the lot. Next, in the Florida town of Stuart, a thirty-year-old woman was arrested for adopting exactly the same childcare methods, although in her case she needed her solitude in order to go bowling and buy alcohol.

Leon Watson, twenty-two, of Albuquerque, USA was arrested for severely beating his two-year-old son. According to Leon, his child had given him the 'mad dog' look as used by gang members staring down rivals.

FAMILY LIFE

It's wonderful to be able to feel secure in the knowledge that someone close to you loves you and is looking out for you …

Teenagers can be so moody. And their parents become a source of huge embarrassment. Take the case of a girl in Tokyo, Japan. Lazy slob father sits down for breakfast and makes a pig of himself: disgusted teenage daughter stabs him in the chest and goes out, leaving him in a pool of blood. 'He won't get out and get a job and the sight of him sitting down and

STRANGE

dad for sale

A debt-ridden Chinese man was desperate enough to sell his father for $1,300 to his own brother. The Shanghai man needed the money to pay for treatment for venereal disease. The sixty-one-year-old father lived with his youngest son and provided something of an income by collecting used plastic bottles, which the son then spent on regular visits to brothels.

making a pig of himself at the breakfast table made me sick,' she was heard to say when she was arrested later in the day at college.

There's a lot to be said for all sitting down together for a family meal. But somehow the effect is lost when the meal consists of the father. Sounds gruesome, we know, but it happened in Sydney, Australia.

Katherine Knight, an abattoir butcher from Sydney, killed and skinned her partner, John Price, then cooked and served him to his family. She left the skin hanging in the hall and the plates in the kitchen, with the names of Price's three children next to them. Earlier, Knight, a forty-four-year-old mother of four, made a home video for her teenage children, outlining plans to slaughter Mr Price, her partner of six years. Then she went to his home, where she found him unconscious, believed to be from a drug overdose, and killed him. Using her abattoir skills and tools she cut off his head and boiled it with body parts and vegetables.

According to one of Mr Price's daughters, he had been planning to end the relationship with Ms Knight, and had already applied for an aggravated violence order against her for fear of what she might do to him. But only one week before his death the couple had been happily sharing a family celebration for a grand-child's birthday, giving absolutely no hint of the horror that was to unfold.

Down, way down in the Deep South of the USA, a fifty-three-year-old man was arrested on a charge of incest. The farm labourer and his sister had set up family unit that had produced nine children and four grandchildren. The family lived in a rural work camp run by the man's employer on the edge of Lake Okeechobee in Florida's Everglades, and their 'keep-it-in-the-family' lifestyle had come to the notice of authorities when a neighbour reported that the couple kept a coffin in their living room in which were the remains of an infant son who had died twelve years earlier.

TWINS

Megan and Caitlin Coleman of Onalaska, USA, are identical twins who both had accidents in the same week. What was weird, in an 'it-could-only-happen-to-identical-twins' way, was that both girls broke their dominant arm in exactly the same place with exactly the same type of break. Because they are mirror twins, which means identicals who have opposite dominant sides, they didn't both break the right arm or left arm, but the 'same' arm nevertheless.

Seventeen-year-old twins Michael and Ashley Good of Christchurch, New Zealand, were caught in mid-burglary. They hailed a cab as their getaway car after emerging from a newsagent's with armfuls of cigarettes, and the taxi-driver drove them straight to the police station. As the sentencing judge pointed out, 'You are halfwits.'

Seventy-year-old twin brothers died within hours of one another after separate accidents on exactly the same road in northern Finland. The first twin died when he was hit by a lorry while riding his bike in Raahe, 600 kilometres north of Helsinki. About two hours later, his brother crossed the same road, also on his bicycle and he too was hit and killed by a lorry. He died just 1.5 kilometres from the spot where his brother was killed. Police in Raahe said it was highly unlikely that the second twin could have known of his brother's death as they had not yet informed the family of the accident.

Australian twin sisters Lake and Flame set up an on-line dating service – the first of its kind – exclusively for twins who want to find love. As Lake pointed out, a lot of twins have trouble in relationships because their partners don't understand the closeness of their twin bond and get jealous. Dating another twin could be the answer.

KIDS – TOUGHER THAN YOU THINK

A three-year-old toddler scampered between parked cars in the centre of Berlin, Germany, and straight into the path of an oncoming vehicle. The little boy, named as Baran, was hit, thrown into the air and when he landed was run over by another vehicle. As doctors said afterwards, he should have been very seriously injured, if not killed – yet he got away with just a scratch on his back. Baran picked himself up and toddled back to his panicking parents as if nothing had happened.

An eleven-month-old baby got stuck in the European Cup when his football-mad father put him in it for a photo. The Barcelona fan was at the club's museum when he put the baby in the replica of the original. It took police and firemen more than twenty minutes to get the baby out. The baby was unharmed but may be left with a pathological fear of major trophies.

A three-week-old infant survived alone for three days in a Chicago apartment after her mother had a heart attack, apparently while changing the baby in the middle of the night. The mother, thirty-five-year-old Virna Mims, who had had heart valve surgery two years earlier, was found lying on the floor next to the bed. Family members reasoned that Mims had placed her infant daughter, Faith, in the middle of the bed to change the nappy when she suffered a heart attack. Concerned at not having heard from her for the three-day period, they went to her apartment, heard the baby crying and called the emergency services. They rushed Faith to hospital where she was found to have suffered nothing more than mild dehydration.

A ROOF OVER ONE'S HEAD

A man turned up at his holiday home in Vermont, USA, to find that squatters had moved in. But as squatters go, they were obviously the sensitive type – they were in the throes of renovating the bathroom, knocking through some walls and repainting the woodwork. All paid for by the sale of some of the property's antiques.

A schoolboy on the remote Scottish Orkney island of Unst has made a few changes to the bus shelter he uses every day. Just to make it a little more like home, he has put down a carpet and moved in a settee, a table and a computer, as well as a fishtank, framed pictures, books and magazines.

When Harry Dennis of Wisconsin, USA, got divorced, leaving him over $2 million poorer, he decided it would make good economic sense to live in the hangar where his twin-engined plane was kept. He installed televisions, a shower, an oven and a fridge, but airport officials said that he was breaking the terms of his lease and after two years of sleeping next to his plane, Harry had to move out.

LIVING ON THE DOORSTEP

An Italian drug dealer sentenced to house arrest spent seven months living on the doormat of his own flat. Except it wasn't his flat any more, it was his old flat, since he had been evicted. Maaouani Ben Ammar, from Milan, was told he would go to jail if he wasn't at his address every day, and did not dare to confess that he had been evicted for non-payment of rent (while he was in custody, of course). So he slept on his doormat and used a neighbour's toilet.

A Singapore woman slept for several weeks on the floor in the corridor outside her own flat because she had locked herself out. Lee Peh Lee slept outside her front door because she was afraid of getting into trouble with her landlord by asking a locksmith to break the lock, and because her husband was working abroad.

HIDDEN AWAY PEOPLE

An emaciated seventy-two-year-old-man was found hiding in the jungle, where he had taken refuge from a war that lasted just 100 hours. Salomon Vides was a migrant worker in Honduras in 1969 when El Salvador invaded. Intervention from the Organisation of American States stopped the war after a few days, but according to Mr Vides, no one told him. He fled into Guatemala, escaped arrest, and thereafter just kept moving, surviving on fruit, fish, roots and turtles. He was eventually discovered in the jungles of Honduras by farmers, to whom he raised his hands in surrender.

A Romanian man hid in a basement for eight years to avoid a three-and-a-half year jail sentence. Thirty-four-year-old Ioan Stoica from Avrig in Sibiu was sentenced for fraud in his absence in 1994. Police officers finally found him hiding in his parents' basement, where he'd secreted himself on learning of his conviction. He will still have to do his time, and may even get a further sentence for evading arrrest.

A Russian army deserter was found by a bear (itself being tracked by hunters) after hiding in a dugout for six years. Viktor Borovik had been in hiding on the Kamchatka peninsula in Russia's Pacific Far East after fleeing the bullying and abuse to which conscripts in the Russian army are subjected. Borovik had been living on fish, berries and mushrooms, and was found when he set fire to his hideout after drinking a bottle of homebrew alcohol. It was the smell of rotting flesh from the burns on Borovik's body that attracted the roaming bear, and the hunters then came across Borovik and took him to hospital.

A soldier was discovered living in the wardrobe of a fifteen-year-old girl's bedroom in Mount Vernon, Ohio, USA. The girl knew about it, mind you, since they were having regular sex and he took photos of her in the nude – on the strength of which Jeffrey Scott Martin, twenty-six, who had deserted from his army unit in Kentucky, was convicted of unlawful sexual conduct. He had met the girl over the internet and secretly moved into her house, living in the wardrobe when her mother was around. It was she who found dishes, a pillow and other items in the wardrobe and concluded that someone was staying there.

One fine day, Vassili Vorobyev simply disappeared. One minute he was there in a little village in the Voronesh region of Russia, working as the assistant manager of a secondary school, with a wife, Tamara; the next he was gone. Tamara reported him missing to the police, but there was absolutely no sign of him anywhere, and in time a rumour began to circulate in the village that he was dead. After a while the school took on a new assistant manager, Tamara got on with her life alone, and gradually Vorobyev faded from people's memories.

A full three years passed before Vorobyev was discovered – in the attic of the school where he used to work. To the astonishment of his wife and the rest of the village, he had been living in total isolation, hiding from the world, for three years, right under their very noses. And if it hadn't been for a few flames from the fire he used to boil potatoes flickering up within sight of the attic window, a villager would not have thought the school was on fire and rushed up to extinguish it, and Vorobyev would be hiding still.

Vorobyev's self-inflicted exile came about after he was called an ignoramus by the school's dierctor. Deeply hurt, and not wishing to be thought stupid, he decided to spend more time studying. But, concerned that his wife might not allow him the free time to spend with his books, he simply stepped away from his life and created a new one in the school attic, where he lived on potatoes and cereals stolen from the school kitchen and pigeons he caught himself. By night he would appropriate school books and firewood and by day he would study mathematics, especially algebra, and sleep. And so passed three years of Vassili Vorobyev's life, as an algebra-loving hermit. His wife forgave him, but we don't know if he forgave the school director who hurt his feelings.

In eastern China's Shandong province, a Mr Wang had a road accident, crashing his car into a truck, killing one person and injuring another. Totally mortified, and in fear of retribution, Mr Wang went home and dug a 4-metre square hole under his bed, and succeeded in hiding there for the next four years. During that time he emerged occasionally at night to buy food. He also managed somehow to get married and father a child.

YOU LUCKY, LUCKY BASTARDS

Some people must have been born with all the right stars in just the right places, and with several gods smiling down on them.

The Core Pacific City Living Mall in Taipei, Taiwan, offered 100 cars in a prize draw as an opening promotion. In eight days Taiwan businessman Hsu Cheng-tao and his wife won six sports utility vehicles, valued at T$430,000 (£8,750) each, after buying new furniture in the mall. They breathed a huge sigh of relief when the draw ended and they were spared the burden of winning yet more cars.

Winning the lottery is lucky. And winning it more than once is very lucky. But winning it three times in three months? A man from New South Wales, Australia, did just that. First he had two winning tickets in one month, winning him a total of about £170,000. Then the next month he bagged a huge £500,000 payout. The man, in his twenties, had bought all three winning tickets from the same newsagent. Which could be the source of his amazing luck – manager Robert

Newton said that he had sold no fewer than twenty-one winning tickets from his shop, with a combined value of about £7 million.

REALLY, REALLY BAD LUCK

They say that you make your own luck, but no one deserves luck like this …

A woman who was allergic to bee stings was stung as she was horse-riding in Middleburg, USA. Janice Ruetz, fifty-two, became disorientated as the bee sting took effect and fell from her horse. Luckily, she had her mobile phone with her and called emergency workers as well as a neighbour for help, while her riding mates also went to seek assistance. Unfortunately, however, Janice had fallen into a part of the road where there were lots of weeds growing, and her neighbour, arriving in a pickup truck did not see her. He ran her over, killing her.

STRANGE

net loss

A fisherman in India found a human head in his net and was sure it was a bad omen. Forty-year-old Baidya Behera of Lalsingh village in Bhanjanagar was fishing in a reservoir when he found the head, and immediately went ashore, hurrying to the nearest temple to pray. When he returned home he was bitten by a poisonous snake and died.

bible belt

In Lins, Brazil, a 3-pound bible was accidentally knocked off the balcony of a twelfth-floor hotel room. It landed squarely on the head of seventy-one-year-old Charles Maurois, sunbathing below, and killed him. Insurers claimed it was an act of God.

A New Zealand man went to feed his pet kitten during a week of heavy frosts, slipped on an icy ramp outside his back door, hit his head and ended up head down in his cat's water bowl. Peter Robinson, twenty-eight, drowned in the 4 centimetres of water in the bowl.

A New Zealand student had two amazing strokes of luck – one good, one not so good. First, he survived a car crash in the rocky hills near Christchurch when his car hit the guard-rail at the side of the road, and managed to hitch a lift to Arthurs Pass to arrange a tow. This is when things went badly wrong for the twenty-two-year-old. Stepping away from the road, where a policeman was helping with the car, to answer a call of nature, he went a little bit too far in his desire for modesty, and plunged to his death into the Otira Gorge.

Anastasia was a prostitute in the Turkish city of Trabzon, with a room on the fifth floor of the Temel Reis Hotel, where her boyfriend worked as a waiter. When, one day, Anastasia's next client fell asleep in his car, she called up her boyfriend, Hakan, so that they could make love. Hakan was up for it, and they were engaged in the act when there was a banging on the door – the sleeping client had woken up and come to see Anastasia. In his panic, Hakan ran to the balcony and tried to climb across to the next room. He grabbed hold of a wire to steady himself and was electrocuted. And if that didn't kill him, the fall from the fifth floor certainly did.

Being a flight attendant is not always easy: spending your working hours in a pressurised, dehydrated, jetlagged state. But at least you can feel safe in the knowledge that you won't get hit by lightning, because the aeroplane takes the strike. According to a recently released medical report, though one hapless flight attendant on an internal American flight had the incredible bad luck to be struck

sh*t happens

When you're at home, sitting on the toilet, you just want a bit of peace and quiet. What you really don't want, is what happened to a woman in Sheerness, Kent, when she was suddenly and explosively covered in excrement from below when water company workers start carrying out high-pressure drain cleaning in the neighbourhood. Yuck.

harder, harder, tighter, tighter

Innocent love play turned into a very unlucky game of death for a Nancy Guzmán of Santiago, Chile. Nancy and her husband Rocco were trying out a bit of erotic asphyxiation, said to greatly enhance orgasm, while they were making love. However, Rocco squeezed too hard on Guzmán's throat and she passed out and died, despite his attempts to resuscitate her. The autopsy revealed that Rocco's attempts to revive her by administering electric shocks from her hairdryer's power lead would have killed her anyway. Rocco was arrested and charged with murder; he was probably choked when he heard the charges read out.

BIZARRE

by lightning as he sat in the rear of the plane. No one else in the plane was remotely affected, and nor was the plane itself. Just that poor attendant, who suffered all the classic symptoms of a full-on lightning strike. An eyewitness saw the man surrounded by a ball of light, with sparks coming off him. That night he experienced nausea, headache, ringing in his ears and numbness in his left arm, and ten weeks later he was still suffering from headaches, insomnia and forgetfulness.

A slumbering teenager had a blast when he rolled over in his sleep on to a can of deodorant, pushing it on to a screwdriver, which punctured it. The escaping aerosol gas was then ignited by a fire in the room and the force of the blast blew out the bedroom windows in Hawksworth, Leeds, as well as injuring the sleepy boy.

SERIAL BAD LUCK

There's a man who works in Düsseldorf, Germany, for a big insurance company in a twenty-six-storey building. And his colleagues won't go in the lift with him. Does he have a flatulence problem? No. Does he tell endless bad jokes? No. But when Karlpeter Arens gets into a lift the chances are it will break down. The hapless Arens has been stuck in lifts no fewer than forty times, starting when he was just six years old and continuing with alarming regularity ever since. These days he tends to walk up and down the stairs. And so do his colleagues.

A Pennsylvania man has refused to go out in the rain after being struck by lightning for the third time in five years. (The odds of being struck three times are several million to one.) Kevin Parent, twenty-four, was first struck in August 1996, then again last year, and most recently was hit by a bolt of lightning while out walking with his three children. Kevin suffered only minor injuries during the three strikes. During the third strike he was pushing his two youngest children in a buggy. He collapsed and suffered temporary memory loss; his wife, Carolynn, says she felt a tingling sensation when her husband leaned against her. He was taken to hospital where doctors found damaged tissue in his blood – a sign that lightning, which packs 35,000 to 40,000 amps, had struck him. 'I've been pretty lucky,' says Mr Parent. 'The next one could kill me.'

How about this for an unbroken chain of bad luck? John Beaumont-Willard and his girlfriend Paula from Worthing decided to get married and to make their planned skiing holiday their honeymoon. First, their flight to Toulouse was held up because the pilot had been taken ill. Not a good omen. Then the bus to Andorra broke down. When they finally got to Andorra and out on to the slopes, John broke his right arm. On the return bus journey they were involved in a crash, and on arrival back home in Worthing they saw first that their car had been broken into and then that their flat had been totally ransacked. Unopened wedding presents had been stolen, and electrical goods, toys and jewellery worth thousands of pounds, as well as family photographs were also stolen. Still, got to look on the bright side: at least they've got their health.

WHAT ARE THE ODDS OF THAT HAPPENING?

Patel, caught Patel, bowled Patel. Cricket umpire Roy Higgins realised he was in for a long and confusing day when he walked on to the field to officiate in a Sunday League match in Bradford. All twenty-two players shared the same surname. Every player, and the scorer too, was called Patel in the match between Yorkshire LPS and Amarmilan. On two earlier occasions when the teams had played there had been twenty-one Patels, but on this day one of the regular players (whose name was not Patel) was absent, and his place was taken by a Mr Patel.

A baby boy beat odds of 160,000–1 when he was born on the same date as his father and grandfather. Andrew Neil was born by Caesarean section on 11 July, exactly thirty-four years after his father David and fifty-four years after his grandfather Robert Lambie.

but you're dead...

Romanians Valeria Richter and her husband had a big row which ended in him threatening to hang himself in the barn, then walking out of the house. Later, Valeria went into the barn to check that he hadn't done anything stupid and was horrified to see a man dangling, lifeless, from a beam. She immediately ran into the nearest town, Arad, to tell the police, then came home to an even bigger shock. There, in their bed, sound asleep, was her husband. Valeria was so astounded at her husband's swift return from the hereafter that she even checked his neck for rope marks, but he hadn't hanged himself: he admitted that he had hidden until she had left for Arad, then went back home and to bed. And the dead man hanging in the barn? Sheer coincidence, said the police, who identified him later.

Andrew was due on 13 July but doctors decided to perform the Caesarean after his heart rate dropped. He was born weighing 7 pounds and his father says the family are looking forward to a huge joint celebration next year.

During family celebrations for her grandparents' fiftieth wedding anniversary, ten-year-old Laura Buxton of Staffordshire released a helium-filled balloon into the sky and watched it drift away; at the very last moment before letting it go she had attached a note to it with her name and address. The balloon travelled 140 miles before coming to rest in a garden in Wiltshire, where another little girl lived. This little girl was also ten years old, and her name was Laura Buxton. Amazed that a balloon from a girl with her name had arrived in her garden, the second Laura Buxton wrote to the first, and it turned out that not only did they have the same name and were the same age, but they both had black labrador dogs (both three years old); they both kept a guinea pig and a rabbit; and they were both blonde-haired. A university statistician later said that the chances of all these things happening were well over a million to one.

Science & Technology

ACADEMIC RESEARCH

We'd all still be living in the Dark Ages if it wasn't for vital work carried out by wonderfully altruistic people given large grants to spend years in libraries and research labs with the sole motivation of making our lives better. Wouldn't we?

Professor Patricia Simonet (Sierra Nevada College, Nevada, USA) discovered a new dog noise. As you know, dogs bark, growl and whine. But, according to Professor Simonet, they also produce an 'idiosyncratic pant' that is joyous and playful, but too subtle for most humans to pick up in the normal run of things. When Professor Simonet played the sound to fifteen puppies, though, they all moved to a play area and began to frolic.

Researchers at the University of Leeds, created a plant that demonstrates when it is under stress by emitting a faint glow. The plant was produced by adding DNA from firefly cells into the mix, enabling it to glow faintly under conditions such as too much heat or not enough light. The next step, presumably, is to breed crops that warn you that they'll underproduce if their conditions don't improve.

Researchers at Kinki University in Nara, Japan, announced that they had successfully bred spinach genes into pigs, producing the first ever mammal-plant combination. They claimed that the meat these spinachy pigs would produce would be healthier than normal pork. Professor Akira Iritani did go on to add, though, that the significance of this scientific breakthrough was more academic than practical.

Pooh-pooh the claims of respected scholars and academics? Never. You'll have to make up your own minds about this one. A scholar claimed to have evidence that men got pregnant in ancient India. Sanskrit teacher Professor Vinod Purani said that his research had uncovered an ancient Hindu scripture containing references to male conception. And as if that wasn't enough, he also said that mention of a man's stomach being cut open to allow a male child to be delivered could refer to the first caesarian. Professor Purani's paper also referred to there being sex changes in ancient India (but if men could change to women, why would men get pregnant? Just a thought).

Dr Michael Bailey, of Northwestern University, Illinois, USA, ran a research project that could have made the earth move (for its subjects, at least). The aim of his research was to determine the sexual arousal rates of females by, respectively, heterosexual erotic images and lesbian erotic images. Women students were paid $75 an hour (two to three times the going rate for campus research guinea pigs) to have a 'vaginal photoplethysmograph' inserted to measure moisture and swelling. Dr Bailey's preliminary conclusion was that women (whether straight or gay) get aroused by either straight or lesbian scenes. Or possibly by having a vaginal photoplethysmograph inserted in them.

 The *Journal of Experimental Biology and Medicine* carried the groundbreaking news that

the time machine?

University of Connecticut physics professor Ronald Mallett, fifty-seven, said that after years of study he may be in a position to begin experiments this year leading to genuine time travel. At first this will involve probably no more than a neutron or two, but it will lay the groundwork for transporting larger objects. Mallett believes his theory, taken from Einstein, is sound, but that amassing the amount of energy necessary even to move small objects may be impossible with current knowledge. Professor Mallett said he's been thinking about time travel since the age of ten, when his father died, because he'd wanted to go back in time and warn his dad of the dangers of smoking. **STRANGE** research now shows that regulating men's hand temperature has no effect on the temperature of the rectum but that regulating scrotal temperature does.

Exploding toads: can humanity save them? Can science find a way? You bet it can. Ask Professor Dietrich Hummel of the Universtiy of Braunschweig in Germany, who has carried out extensive (and, dare we say, expensive?) research in a state-of-the-art wind tunnel to show that a car passing over a toad on the road at over 20 mph can cause it to explode. Using this research Professor Hummel is calling for speed limits to be imposed on toad-crossing black spots, although, as he points out, speed is not the only factor – clearance height makes a difference too. Heaven forbid that a Formula 1 car should drive over a toad, he said.

IT MAY LOOK ANCIENT ...

Experts had long been puzzling over some mysterious rock formations in the south Saskatchewan River region of Canada. Hundreds of stones were stacked in ways that suggested ancient burial mounds, or perhaps a sacred site for the native cultures. Finally, a Mrs Sara Burd rang the local newspaper in Medicine Hat to admit that her father had built the formations when he was trying to get over his broken marriage.

Way back in 1898, a farmer uncovered a stone on his land in Kensington, Minnesota, USA. The stone had runes inscribed on it, and fuelled a belief that

Norsemen had been in North America in the fourteenth century, well before Columbus crossed the Atlantic. The Kensington Stone, as it was called, became the subject of much academic debate as to its authenticity. Then, when rock carvings were found last year which also appeared to be Viking writings, it began to seem as though the Kensington Stone really was a true record of Norse presence in Minnesota. As the University of Minnesota started to ask people to make contributions toward the cost of scientific testing, two academics, graduates of the university could bear it no longer. Kari Ellen Gade, now chairwoman of the Department of Germanic Studies at Indiana University, and Jana Schulman, associate professor of English at Southeastern Louisiana University, came forward to say that they had made the carvings in 1985 when they were students, 'for fun', and to cast doubts on the validity of the original Kensington Runestone.

CYBERODDITIES

The quest for knowledge drives technology. But once the knowledge has been acquired, the technology is still around, and it starts to be used in ways that could not have been predicted.

Only in Silicon Valley. Sequoia Hospital launched a scheme in which new-born babies get an e-mail address within seconds of seeing the light of day. Cybersavvy parents can get their kids wired to the world with e-mail and a personalised domain name, while the parents get on-line tips and resources for childcare and parenting. Sequoia Hospital were proud to be able to say that they were the first to offer this service – a fun way to welcome babies to the twenty-first century.

The anguished cries of a distressed bird led to firemen searching for over an hour in an office block in Willenhall in the West Midlands. The source of the noise turned out to be a toucan screensaver.

You know you have to see five-second time-lapse pictures of your pet when you're separated from it. So the owners of pet boarding kennels in West Boldon, South Tyneside have set up web-cams for this very purpose.

According to Islamic law any written message concerning divorce is binding. So when a twenty-six-year-old woman received a text message on her mobile phone from her angry husband saying, 'Why are you late? You are divorced,' the marriage was deemed by a court to be annulled. The couple are continuing to live together, however.

A truly great icon, and a landmark of the cyber-age was auctioned off, going to a German web publisher for £3,350. The object in question was a coffee pot – the coffee pot that attracted fans around the world when it starred for one of the first ever web-cams. Originally put on-line so that scientists working in distant Cambridge University labs could see whether

WEIRD

cybercheats

Bored with his marriage, a Beijing man entered an internet chatroom in search of passion. His wife, who was apparently equally bored, was doing the same thing. Anyway, he soon found someone with whom to share his passion and arranged to meet her, while his wife similarly set up a discreet rendezvous for herself. They arrived for their respective dates carrying a rolled-up newspaper for identification and saw that they had set themselves up with each other. The resultant fight was so savage that police had to tear them apart.

there was a brew happening or whether it needed a refill, the legendary filter machine became a daily focal point for Netizens round the world. The coffee pot was replaced after ten years of faithful service in favour of a snazzy new espresso machine, and is no longer operational. But the journalists of the on-line edition of *Der Spiegel* felt it was a crucial part of internet history and worth every penny.

Women in Poland have begun signing up for mobile phone text messages warning them when not to have sex. It's all based on the rhythm method, a very popular means of contraception in 90 per cent Catholic Poland. After entering details about their menstrual cycle, the women would then receive messages at the most fertile time in their cycle warning them to abstain from sex.

A big internet success in the UK in the last year or so has been a site called 'Friends Reunited', through which people can contact old schoolmates. Just in fun, Mike Breach and Chris Harvey set up a similar site called 'Convicts Reunited', but to their great surprise it attracted thousands of users from around the world, with registered ex-cons in the database now numbering 3,000. So it looks as though Mike and Chris are going to have to take it a little bit more seriously.

Kay Hammond, of Birmingham attempted to push back the boundaries of the internet and get a husband at the same time. The twenty-four-year-old internet entrepreneur auctioned herself as a wife, with a £250,000 reserve price, on the auction site eBay, with bidders to be aged between twenty-four and thirty-five. The high reserve price was designed to guarantee that someone from the business world would offer his hand. Bids then proceeded to soar as high as £10 million, but proved to be hoaxes. So no cyberhubby for Kay.

A ladies' knitting club in Britain suffered verbal abuse as fans of shock rock group Slipknot bombarded its website with threatening e-mails. Fans of the American nu-metal group felt that the knitters' quarterly journal, also called Slipknot, could be confused with their idols and sent e-mails telling them they shouldn't be on the internet with that name. Rita Taylor, chair of the Knitting and Crochet Guild, said the e-mails were very disturbing. 'But we are not going to let it bother us.' She said the thousand or so middle-aged members of the guild have little in common with the American thrash group, who call their fans 'maggots'.

INVENTIONS

A German designer has created a soup bowl with a tilted bottom. It stands on the table like a normal bowl, and the soup collects at one side. Claus Roeting from Osnabruck invented the dish to solve the etiquette problem of tilting the dish manually, and hopes demand for it will come from all the high-class restaurants.

A husband-and-wife inventing team came up with a cushion which muffles farts and stops them from smelling too. (They've even tested it after a sausage and beans dinner to make sure.) The gas-absorbing cushion contains a filter which lasts six

steamy scandinavian meetings

A Finnish company has designed a sauna with video-conferencing facilities. Company head Jarkko Lumio said his executives already use the sauna regularly, so Media Tampere's creation features a web camera and microphone inside, and a window looking out on to a computer screen. The sauna fits four. Mr Lumio said it is up to them what they wear, but Finnish tradition is to sauna in the nude.

ring of confidence

OK, remember Olestra? The non-fattening oil that didn't get metabolised but just ran straight through you? So Americans could carry on eating fatty foods and not get too obese? Well, it didn't do so well in the end because it caused 'anal leakage' and 'faecal urgency'. Now, however, with the invention of the Neosphincter, such incontinence problems may be a thing of the past. The Food and Drug administration in the USA has approved the artificial sphincter, which has had a good success rate in people trained in its use; but it's not as yet for public sale, since in trials with untrained users there were too many 'adverse incidents'.

WEIRD

months for a woman, and three for a man. Co-creator Jim Huza, from Greenville, North Carolina, USA, produced the GasBGon cushion in a variety of eye-catching designs after his wife Sharron came up with the idea as a notional scheme for her marketing class. Huza claims the cushion can absorb almost anything a fart can throw at it.

Swiss inventor Paolo Rais came up with the ultimate solution to the boring dinner party. No longer, if they eat at his table, will unlucky guests end up stuck next to the dinner-party bore. The Paolo Rais dining table has moving chairs with a wooden tray that holds your meal. The chairs move at a rate of 3 inches per minute, guaranteeing that no diner spends more than ten minutes next to the same person.

A Dutch furniture company has designed an armchair that pours a glass of whisky for its occupant. The Original Whisky Chair spurts its cargo from a lion's head at the end of an armrest. It boasts a 2-litre reservoir, as well as a childproof mechanism. The alcohol reservoir can be filled with other drinks, of course, and Dirk van der Velden, director of the Twentse Furniture Company of Oldenzaal, said it can be upholstered with whatever the customer wants. The chair was the brainchild of Scotsman Ron Ferris.

According to University of Nebraska geologist John Shroder, an Afghanistan specialist, the Pentagon has developed a Remote-Sensing Gas-Detection Device so finely tuned that it can distinguish

the incredible shrinking shirt

Fashion house Corpo Nove of Florence, Italy, developed a shirt that rolls up its own sleeves. The fabric, which is made of a mix of fibres that includes titanium and other metals, can 'remember' certain shapes. The shirt has been programmed to shrink from wrist to elbow when the temperature rises by a few degrees. When the wearer then goes into a cooler room the shirt will take only about a minute to regain its original shape. **BIZARRE** ethnic groups based on the faint aromas of the foods that they eat.

Human food and drink tasters are all very well, but even the keenest palates become jaded after while. Antonio Ruil of São Carlos, Brazil, has invented a robotic tongue so good at its job that it could easily replace professional food tasters. The handheld electronic tongue rivals human taste buds in accuracy but, unlike a real tongue, never loses its edge. It can even tell the difference between two different wines from the same winery but from different years.

Using state-of-the-art global positioning technology, researchers at the University of Bristol, are on the verge of developing a wrist-worn computer that guides its wearer to the nearest pub. The machine even gives a short description of the pub, as well as noting how far away it is.

Everyone goes to the toilet, and in Germany people usually spend between fifteen and twenty minutes there. Which is why Georges Hemmerstoffer, whose company prints advertisements on toilet paper, has decided to add classic works of literature to their output. Georges seized his opportunity with authors like Romantic poet Heinrich Heine whose copyright has expired, while one contemporary German author actually approached Hemmersteffer asking for his books to be printed on toilet rolls. The books will be printed in instalments so that a twelve-chapter book, for example, will fit perfectly into a twelve-roll multi-pack.

Two California entrepreneurs came up with a new consumer product: Nicotine Water. One bottle of water contains the same amount of nicotine as two cigarettes, but without the tar and other carcinogens. Apparently, Nicotine Water tastes just like plain mineral water, and not, as you might think, of cigarette ends soaked in water. The idea was based on some research showing that nicotine boosts the memory. The producers hope it will become popular in the many places in California where smoking is banned, like restaurants, night-clubs and gyms.

ENERGY FROM EXCREMENT

Hindu nationalists in Gujarat, India began promoting cow's urine as a health cure, selling it at 30p a bottle under the name 'Gift of the Cow'. The healing properties of cow dung and cow's urine are mentioned in ancient Hindu texts and authorities claim that the urine can cure anything from skin diseases, and kidney and liver ailments to obesity, heart ailments and even cancer. Vidhyaben Mehta, a sixty-five-year-old woman with a cancerous tumour on her chest who has been taking cow's urine for the past three years, says she is no longer in pain and has survived in spite of medical predictions that she would die two years ago.

this beer tastes like shit

Archaeologists uncovered what they believed to be a 5,000-year-old pub and brewery on the remote Scottish islands of Orkney, and following the ancient recipe, brewed a beer flavoured with animal dung. Merryn Dineley, from Manchester University, was chief brewer of the Stone Age ale and insisted it was delicious.

STRANGE

It was announced that Britain would have its first dung-fired power station. Thirty farmers in Devon got ready to provide about 1.6 million tons of slurry a year, which is stored and fermented to produce 'biogas' to drive turbines and provide electricity and hot water to heat local schools, hospitals and homes.

Thailand's energy policy office announced plans to get more value from its prison population's debt to society by turning their excrement into gas. After a successful nationwide campaign to turn pig dung into gas, authorities sought new sources of energy to reduce dependency on costly imported fossil fuels. Thailand's prisons hold some 240,000 inmates, which adds up to plenty of poo for biogas production.

The water supply in the Bolivian capital city of La Paz runs through an abandoned mine and is polluted, picking up harmful iron and cadmium particles. To counteract the problem, filters made from llama dung have been developed to purify the water. Scientists say that the droppings provide the perfect home for those bacteria that remove the toxic metals from the water.

CROSSED WIRES

Telephone companies do get their lines crossed, and odd things happen.

Bonnie Johnson was stuck in a lift for an hour between floors in a New Plymouth tax office, on New Zealand's North Island, but when she used the lift's emergency phone her call was routed to a newspaper office 500 miles away on the South Island. Joan Pankhurst, the manager of the *Southland Times*, called the New Plymouth emergency services then spent the rest of the time reassuring Bonnie that help was on the way. A thunderstorm was thought to have jumbled the tax office's telephone numbers.

hot line

German telephone company Deutsche Telekom made a bit of a mess of reassigning old telephone numbers. One error was giving the old number of the German Medical Council to a sex line. So doctors calling up the council's information service were greeted with the seductive, sultry voice of a very naughty nurse hoping to raise the caller's temperature.

Customers who phoned a US electricity company's helpline got help that they may not have been looking for. A letter that Green Mountain Energy sent to 93,000 customers in Pennsylvania gave the wrong number for its customer service department, and the customers got through to a sex line offering wild one-on-one adventures. Hundreds of customers complained about the message (out of 93,000 ...?), and Green Mountain Energy went into negotiation with the owner of the sex line, PrimeTel Communications, to buy the number.

Nutty as a Fruitcake

OBSESSIONS – WEIRD BY DEFINITION

Some people manage to contract a one-man epidemic of morbid interest in a topic or activity. Bees never buzzed more frantically than in the bonnets of these people ...

Indian police arrested a man for threatening to kill a tiger he believed to be his lover from a previous life. He claimed that Rani, a white tigress, had come to him in a dream and asked him to take her away from the zoo in Hyderabad. Himanshu Das had been seen the previous day in front of Rani's cage, pleading with her to look him in the eyes, and he took her refusal to do so as proof that she didn't want to come with him back to Calcutta. After shouting abuse at Rani, he went back to his hotel, called the zoo and announced that he was going to have to kill her.

There are many paths to enlightenment, but I bet you hadn't thought of cutting up mustard seeds as being one of them. Sebastian David from southern

India cut a mustard seed into 508 pieces with a razor blade, taking sixteen minutes to do so, and claimed that it is a practice which takes the mind into a higher plane. His interest in cutting small things into even smaller pieces was fired by a Bangalore man who cut a cucumber into 100,000 pieces.

John Rutland travels on the Portsmouth to Gosport ferry about twenty-two times every week in his spare time. He says he enjoys every single one of the half-mile crossings, as each one is different in its own way, and he especially likes a heavy swell and rough seas. A return ticket costs £1.60, so you can work out roughly how much John has spent in reaching his remarkable 14,000 tally to date.

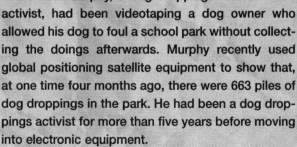

get a life, patrick

Fifty-year-old Patrick Murphy of Boulder, Colorado, USA, was acquitted of harassment by a jury who heard how Murphy, a dog droppings activist, had been videotaping a dog owner who allowed his dog to foul a school park without collecting the doings afterwards. Murphy recently used global positioning satellite equipment to show that, at one time four months ago, there were 663 piles of dog droppings in the park. He had been a dog droppings activist for more than five years before moving into electronic equipment.

next stop, the jungle

A San Diego computer programmer who has spent
£100,000 on tattoos and plastic surgery to turn
himself into a tiger was working on a fur graft as his
next step towards total tigerness. He is tattooed
from head to toe with orange and black stripes; his
teeth have been filed to sharp points and his nails
shaped into claws; he has had latex whiskers
implanted, and surgery to his lips has given him a
permanent feline snarl. Oh, and he changed his
name by deed poll from Dennis Smith (not very tiger-
ish) to Cat Man. Cat Man has a collection of old tiger
pelts and was aiming to have them surgically applied
to his body in a perma-wig. Since he was still holding down his $80,000-a-year programming job, he
had the funds to pay for this $100,000 operation.

yule have to stop

A man in west Wiltshire has such a fondness for the feelings, tastes and smells associated with that very special time of year that he has celebrated Christmas every single day for the last ten years. Andy Park has a decorated tree, eats a full turkey-and-trimmings dinner and even watches a video of the Queen's speech on a daily basis. Over the past decade Andy's Yulemania has cost him a total of £100,000, not to mention the fact that his turkey dinners have him weighing in at a dangerous 19 stone (120 kilograms). Sadly, since he now faces bankruptcy, the Christmas party could well be over.

Wilmer Granda Vega is a man with a vision (all right, an obsession). He's not married yet but he definitely wants the woman he weds to share that vision, to the point of making her sign a legal prenuptial document in which she will agree to have twelve children. Vega, twenty-eight, is an acrobat, and his vision is to form his own family circus. Since Vega performs as a clown, trick motorcyclist, trapeze artist, magician and dancer, he'll certainly be able to teach his kids the skills – as long as he finds the right woman first.

Carnival! Pulsating rhythms, outlandish costumes, funky music … But sixty-seven-year-old Helmut Scherer, who lives in the non-carnival-celebrating

German town of Paderborn, celebrates carnival all by himself, and has been doing so ever since he first moved there in 1956. Each year he creates a new costume and parades through the streets, receiving the key to the city hall from the mayor at the start of his parade. Helmut now has a forty-three-strong fan club of people who line the streets (as much as forty-three people can line streets, that is) to watch him celebrate.

It may not be everyone's idea of a worthwhile inheritance, but a man from Weybridge in Surrey was the recipient in his grandmother's will of her vast collection of over 6,000 pencil erasers.

It was only a movie, it wasn't real life, but that didn't stop a Japanese woman being obsessed with the Coen brothers' 1996 film *Fargo*, a black comedy in which a character takes ransom money and buries it in a snowdrift in the barren Minnesota back country. Takako Konishi, twenty-eight, was taken to the police in Bismarck, North Dakota, after she was found hunting around in a dump. She showed police a crude treasure map she had drawn based on the movie and explained that she had come from Tokyo to search for the cache of money. She then travelled to Fargo and on to Detroit Lakes, 45 miles away, then hitched a ride to a place outside town where she thought the money was hidden. That was the last time she was heard of alive. Her body was found by a hunter, and the cause of death was not known.

Peter Holden, from Washington DC, eats an average of two McDonald's meals every day, and has

he asda be crazy

ODD

A pensioner has spent £18,000 in petrol visiting every Asda supermarket in Britain over the last twelve years. Richard Bunn of Weston-super-Mare arranged his holidays around ensuring that he covered all 250 stores. The seventy-seven-year-old has clocked up 120,000 miles in his E-registered (1988 model) Austin Maestro and says he now plans to visit Asda's American Wal-Mart stores.

eaten at over 11,000 McDonald's in North America. On a recent fifty-four-day business trip he managed to visit 125 of the golden-arched hamburger restaurants, and describes himself as a 'collector of the McDonald's dining experience'. Thirty-nine-year-old Holden has even made the trip to have his hair cut at the McDonald's company barber at HQ in Oak Brook, Illinois. There are over 13,500 McDonald's in North America, so Holden still has plenty of work to do to bag the lot.

Identical twins Ruth and Rebecca Brown are students at Messiah College in Pennsylvania, USA, and came to the attention of weird media for having created 4,386 tiny but highly detailed clay cats wearing Union and Confederate clothing. It's all part, they said, of their fascination with Civil War battlefields. But cats?

At the time of writing, South African Lara Johnstone was a couple of months into a hunger strike in the United States. Her cause? To make President George W. Bush embrace the idea that alien life exists in space. Lara feels very strongly that space-based weapons should be banned, and that space exploration should be undertaken in co-operation with all cultures on earth and in space. This is Lara's second hunger strike, and she has said that this time it will be to the death, if need be.

Gordon Campbell has not missed a single match of his team, Stirling Albion, for eighty-one years, home or away, and has now watched no fewer than

3,000 consecutive games. The ninety-year-old retired butcher started in 1920, and even joined the RAF during the Second World War (when there were no games) to fight back at the Luftwaffe, who had bombed the Stirling stadium.

A Dutch man named only as Nicholas G. was given a two-week suspended sentence for collecting female urine from public toilets at Rotterdam airport. Nicholas is obsessed with women's wee; in fact he gets a sexual thrill from it. He collected the urine in bags which he'd placed in the ladies' loos, after summoning up Dutch courage to enter the toilets by downing a few beers (otherwise he wouldn't have had the bottle). His girlfriend (yes, he was in a relationship at the time) told the court that Nicholas was too scared of HIV and AIDS (but clearly not of public toilets) to have a sexual relationship with her, but he still wanted contact with women; Nicholas said he had given up on the pee thing and was watching porn films instead.

Steven Spielberg's megahit *ET* was re-released in 2002 to mark its twentieth anniversary. That's not the weird part of this story, by the way. The weird part is sci-fi -mad Sian Thurkettle, who at the time of writing had seen the film 773 times. Sian, from Rugby, first saw the film on its original release in 1982 and from then on 'couldn't get enough of it'. She watches it on video at least once a fortnight and says that she cries every time. The re-release was good news for her and to make the most of it she bought a month-long pass

STRANGE

ancient elvis

Finnish musician Jukka Ammondt has achieved cult status for his recordings of Elvis Presley songs translated into Latin. His latest release goes back even further into the depths of linguistic history, being 'Blue Suede Shoes' sung in ancient Sumerian (translated for him by Professor Simo Parpola). The refrain 'You can do anything, but don't step on my blue suede shoes' becomes, as most of you who know Sumerian will already have worked out, 'Nig-na-me-si ib-ak-ke-en e-sir-kus-za-gin-gu ba-ra-tag-ge-en'.

for her local cinema. Sian has also collected more than eighty ET figures and 300 items bearing the extra-terrestrial's image.

Two fans (remember, 'fan' is short for 'fanatic') of the *Star Wars* film series began queuing outside a cinema in Seattle, USA, to make sure of good seats when the new movie *Attack of the Clones* came to the cinema. John Guth and Jeff Tweitem started queuing on New Year's Day 2002 for a release scheduled for the month of May, meaning that they had a five-month wait on their hands.

In 1966, when Irv Gordon, a middle-school science teacher, was twenty-five he went into a Volvo showroom on Long Island, New York, USA, and took a new coupé out for a test drive. He loved it so much that he stayed out for three hours, returning when the car was out of fuel, and decided he had to have it, despite the fact that it cost nearly a year's salary. It was the beginning of a true obsession. Irv drove that Volvo out of the showroom on a Friday evening and drove the whole weekend, clocking up the

bear knuckle fighter

In June 1997 Troy Hurtubise, a scrap-metal dealer from North Bay, Ontario, was so obsessed with grizzly bears that he embarked on a ten-year, $100,000 project to build a suit that would withstand the attack of a grizzly. The project brought him bankruptcy, but he continued to pursue his dream with uncommon determination. Forward to the present day, and a suit he built from rubber, steel and titanium underwent a battery of tests and passed them all: assaults with baseball bats and even being crushed under a lorry had no effect on either suit or Troy inside it. But the suit needed further developments before it would allow him to face the ultimate test, and his long-awaited Ursus mark VI suit was tested at a special facility in British Columbia. Hurtubise hung the suit in a cage with a 1,200 pound Kodiak bear, which promptly ripped it apart. In a quick switch to a back-up suit, Hurtubise then spent ten minutes face-to-face with a small female grizzly bear. He left, promising that he would carry on toughening the suit in order to go face-to-face with a Kodiak.

1,500 miles – and when he drove back to the dealership on Monday morning for the car's 1,500-mile service, they just couldn't believe it. That was in 1966, and it wasn't a flash in the pan or a short-term love affair. By 1987 Irv had driven his beloved Volvo 1 million miles. Now, as of March 2002, Irv has just exceeded 2 million miles in his cherry-red Volvo P1800. The seat is original, though it's been re-covered twice with new leather. The engine was rebuilt once, at 680,000 miles. The car has rewarded his love by never breaking down. At sixty-one, Irv is still driving it and, who knows, he may even cover 3 million miles in it.

WEIRD VOICES INSIDE WEIRD HEADS

A triple gold medallist was kicked out of the Winter Olympics in Salt Lake City, Utah, USA, for failing a drugs test. But he claimed he had been told what to do by aliens. Cross-country skier Johann Muehlegg said the mysterious beings were having a profound effect on his life. 'I have seen them,' he declared, before insisting that he had not taken drugs. German-born Muehlegg defected to Spain in 1999 – on the instructions of the aliens. He was contacted, he said, and told what to do by people from the other side. Whether you believe him or not, it certainly paid off, since he became Olympic champion. Muehlegg failed a second dope test but was only ordered to hand back one of his gold medals for the 50 kilometres. The International Olympic Committee had no power to seize the medals for the 10- and 30-kilometre events because they took place before he was tested.

The Alaska Court of Appeals ruled that a judge could not take away a man's gun permit just because the man in question believed that he had been injected with deadly chemicals and that a computer chip was planted in his head. The man, Timothy Wagner, came to the attention of authorities when he entered a store in Anchorage dripping wet because he was trying to soak the aforementioned deadly chemicals out of his body. He was carrying a loaded .357 handgun (fully licensed) with him.

Marvin Martin II went on trial in Ottawa, Ohio, USA, accused of shooting and killing a fifteen-year-old boy following an incident with the boy's mother. Mr Martin II insisted that the man who carried out the crime was not him but his clone. And in fact, he said, it could have been one of three clones, since he had been cloned three times while in the US Army. But if he's Marvin Martin the second, couldn't that mean he really had been cloned ...

The Hollywood actress Nicole Kidman was unlucky enough to be stalked, by a man named Matthew Hooker. (Hooker was warned by a judge that he would be jailed if he went within 250 yards of Kidman.) But in a bizarre twist, Hooker claimed that he himself was the object of a stalker, and that his stalker was none other than Hollywood actor Ben Affleck.

elvis lives, has headaches

Dr Donald Hinton, a psychiatrist in Independence, Missouri, USA, reasserted his claim that he regularly treats Elvis for migraine headaches. According to Dr Hinton, Elvis still sings, but he no longer shakes his hips because he has arthritis. Now white-haired, as a sixty-seven-year-old would very probably be, the King phones Dr Hinton and has even given him things that can be tested for his DNA. Dr Hinton says that Elvis goes under the name of Jessie (the name given to his twin brother who died at birth) and that the book he has written called *The Truth About Elvis Aaron Presley* was actually co-written with Elvis himself.

According to Hooker, Affleck was stalking him because he was afraid that he would be chosen ahead of him for a film role. Mostly, he says, Affleck has only waved at him from a passing car, but once he followed him dressed as a Frenchman, with a toothbrush moustache.

DELUSIONS OF GRANDEUR

A twenty-eight-year-old from Tulln who had spent a good deal of his working life as a cleaner at dental surgeries in Vienna, Lower Austria and Burgenland believed that he'd seen enough to know what to do, and decided it was time for him to move up in the world. So he set up his own dental practice. Over the years he had managed to steal dental supplies, and when he saw a set of second-hand dental equipment, including drills, in a newspaper ad, he bought it. The final piece in the jigsaw fell into place when he acquired a certificate of qualification, stolen from a dental surgery which he used to get a licence.

The unnamed man had signed up hundreds of patients and treated at least sixty-one of them at his practice before police caught up with him. He was arrested following a string of complaints from patients, including fourteen from people whose teeth were permanently damaged.

Plain Stupid

I HAVE NO RECOLLECTION OF THAT ...

An eighty-three-year-old man left his home in the Cheddar area of Somerset, to go to the barber's for a haircut. He drove away at 9 a.m. on a Monday, and

going, going, gone (his memory)

An auctioneer from Maine, USA, spent seventy-two days away from home after popping out to buy some coffee. Sixty-five-year-old Claude Van Tassel hadn't the faintest idea where he'd been or how he had survived with no money for over ten weeks, and his family had given him up for dead. Mr Van Tassel was found when investigators tracked him down to a homeless shelter in Davenport, Iowa, over 500 miles away from home, still dressed in the same checked shirt and blue trousers he had been wearing on the day he left. At first, when he was put in touch with his nearest and dearest he didn't recognise them, but it slowly dawned on him who they were and he was returned to the bosom of his family.

ODD

found himself at 2 p.m. on Tuesday more than 130 miles away in a pub – with no recollection of how he had got there (and without a haircut).

This case has really got the experts baffled: a New Yorker went out to buy a loaf of bread on 25 July 1969. Carl Hoede finally came home after thirty-two years (whether or not he was clutching a decomposed loaf of bread is unknown) with absolutely no recollection of where he had been, and totally unaware that he had been away for over three decades. Carl, now fifty-seven, thought that Richard Nixon was still president of the USA, and that the Vietnam War was still going on, and he spoke of the moon landings by American astronauts as if this were a very recent event.

VICTIMS TOO STUPID TO DESERVE OUR SYMPATHY

You have to admire the spunk of the two perpetrators, and shake your head slowly at the depths of credulity exhibited by the victims in this case. Two inmates at Cook County jail in the US state of Illinois managed to swindle money out of no fewer than twelve people by calling them at random from the jail premises and promising to cleanse their non-existent criminal records for a fee. The people they called were stupid enough first to accept a reverse charge call from a complete stranger, and second not to have clocked the security message that broke into the calls every sixty seconds to point out that the call was being made from a jail. Oh and third, in the case of one woman, to cough up $9,000 for the 'service'.

 You'd think that someone who worked in a bank would have more than a passing acquaintance with their own country's currency, wouldn't you? Some might say it was a prerequisite for the job. Well, the highest denomination banknote ever printed in the USA was a $100,000 note, and currently there is nothing higher than a $100 bill. So it is a little alarming that when a woman presented a $1 million note at a bank in Harrisburg, Pennsylvania, in order to open an account, the bank clerk took it without question. Guess what? That $1 million bill was forged.

The woman later withdrew some of it and transferred it to another account, before eventually being charged with deception (deception of the very stupid, probably).

You'd might imagine that it would only happen in a cheesy comedy film, and anyway that no one would be idiotic enough to do it. It would be like buying the Eiffel Tower or the Empire State Building. But … in Bucharest, Romania's capital city, a lawyer and his accomplice succeeded in selling part of the country's United States Embassy. The two agreed a £3.5m price for a third of the building with a Romanian businessman. Police uncovered the scam when the poor buyer actually tried to move into his new luxury 'home' in Bucharest.

Scott Boyes of Dunstable had got himself a new book and sat down in a park to start reading it.

Now since the book was *Helping Yourself with Self Hypnosis* you might be able to guess what would happen next (although Scott clearly didn't). He began to feel ver-eee sleee-peee, his eyelids felt ver-eee

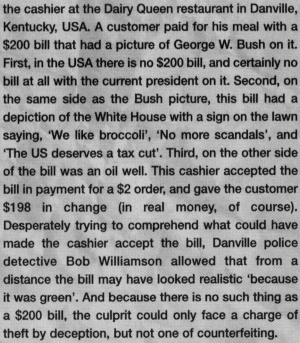

conned by a cartoon

If there was a competition for the most stupid cashier in the world – and who's to say there won't be one day? – then our nomination would be for the cashier at the Dairy Queen restaurant in Danville, Kentucky, USA. A customer paid for his meal with a $200 bill that had a picture of George W. Bush on it. First, in the USA there is no $200 bill, and certainly no bill at all with the current president on it. Second, on the same side as the Bush picture, this bill had a depiction of the White House with a sign on the lawn saying, 'We like broccoli', 'No more scandals', and 'The US deserves a tax cut'. Third, on the other side of the bill was an oil well. This cashier accepted the bill in payment for a $2 order, and gave the customer $198 in change (in real money, of course). Desperately trying to comprehend what could have made the cashier accept the bill, Danville police detective Bob Williamson allowed that from a distance the bill may have looked realistic 'because it was green'. And because there is no such thing as a $200 bill, the culprit could only face a charge of theft by deception, but not one of counterfeiting.

heav-eee, and before long he was fast asleep. When he awoke his mobile phone and two shirts he had just bought were gone. Apparently it's the brighter people who go under more easily – but there are always exceptions.

This story brings to mind those jokes about stupid people betting on the outcome of action replays because they didn't think it could happen the same way twice. Except this wasn't a joke. Bryan Allison, twenty-four, of Buffalo, USA, was injured after falling 20 feet to the ground while hurling a television set off the second-floor balcony at his home. It would appear that Allison was watching a videotape of a 1989 National Hockey League playoff game with his brother. He'd seen it before, but that didn't stop him from dissolving into a rage when his team lost – again. He picked up the TV set and attempted to toss it off the balcony but apparently failed to let go of it in time.

Now there's a film with which you may be familiar called *Speed*, in which a bus carrying a load of passengers has to be driven above a certain speed to prevent a bomb from going off. That was a story; fiction; made up. But when a passenger jumped from a taxi in Austin, Texas, USA, and told the driver that if he stopped a bomb would go off, the driver actually took it at face value and proceeded to drive for an hour and a half non-stop through the city centre. Police eventually persuaded him to stop his cab, which did not then explode, and neither were any explosives found in the cab.

A Florida, USA, man was imprisoned after injuring his hand with a home-made grenade he used to protect himself from muggers. Richardo Gonzalez of Fort Lauderdale was sensibly carrying four home-made bombs in his bag – to scare off potential robbers – when one of them exploded. He then wisely picked another one out of his bag and while he was holding it, that one exploded too. The police soon arrived to arrest him and a bomb squad was called to safely detonate the two remaining grenades. Gonzalez was charged with bomb-making.

ABUSING THE EMERGENCY SERVICES

Emergency services in Oxfordshire received a call from a seven-year-old boy, following an incident in which his mum refused to give him egg on toast for breakfast because he had been a naughty boy.

Dina Pascoe-Stevens from the east of England is a heavy user of the ambulance services. It has been revealed that she phones the emergency services on average twice a day to get them to do vital things like fetching milk from the fridge. In one month she called an ambulance forty times and the police seventeen times, while the fire brigade got off lightly with just three calls. Miss Pascoe-Stevens, who lives in assisted accommodation, says that her carers don't always put things where she wants them so she phones the emergency services for help.

what did you say the problem was?

This year, in an attempt to reduce the number of pointless calls on their valuable time, the London Ambulance Service released a round-up of some the worst abuses of the emergency services: one man had dialled 999 because he couldn't dance and another because he said he felt sick after picking his nose then eating jam from the end of his finger; a woman called the ambulance for her husband because he wouldn't listen to her; and one caller had rung up the emergency services from his mobile phone to check the number of his home phone.

Firefighters in Uganda answered an emergency call only to discover that the caller wanted them to wash urine from his limo. The foreign diplomat had been drinking in a Kampala club, and when he came out, he found a man urinating against his car. The firefighters refused to clean the car for him and immediately headed back to their station.

ARE THESE THINGS ALIVE?

The foot-and-mouth crisis in the UK during the summer of 2001 caused concern overseas as well as in Britain. Fear of infection affected *The Scotsman*'s chess correspondent, John Henderson, who landed in Seattle, USA, and was discovered by customs officials to have a haggis in his luggage. They took the poor haggis out on to the runway and shot it repeatedly, then soaked it in petrol.

Another foot-and-mouth scare caused a three-month delay to the wedding of Gareth Moore and Karen Wood in Australia. Gareth is originally from Wales, and had his ceremonial Welsh sporran flown out especially for the occasion. But customs officials seized it and quarantined it, giving it three weeks of irradiation treatment for good measure.

SHIRKING RESPONSIBILITY

A postman in Japan was sacked after stashing 1,100 letters at his home because he couldn't be bothered to deliver them. All the letters, which had been cached over a fourteen-year period, had been sent to addresses that were new to him, and whose location he didn't know. He hadn't wanted to ask colleagues where these addresses were in case they would think he was useless. Which, of course, they do now.

Another postie who didn't deliver was twenty-five-year-old Graham Fletcher of Edinburgh, Scotland, who was discovered to have stashed away 696 items of mail that should have gone out to the good people of Edinburgh. Graham had received something of a shock one night when he decided to surprise his wife, who was (supposedly) out on a ladies-only night, only to find her engaged in a sex act up against a van. This apparently led to him sinking into depression and hoarding mail as a 'cry for help'.

Hmmm, how do I get out of my National Service? Well, if I was married with a kid, I'd get a two-year suspension of my call-up. So, with this in mind, a resourceful Russian conscript used his last day before going into military service very wisely indeed. With just twenty-four hours to go before the train came to take him away to a military unit, the Russian teenager from Yakutsk in Siberia got married and adopted a small child. (And if he has another child within the next two years he will be permanently exempt.) Shame really ... that sort of resourcefulness and initiative would be useful in the Army ...

A thousand people had to be evacuated from their homes in an army base in Blandford, Dorset, because a woman didn't want to go to work. Catherine Matchett, who worked in the army base's pub, placed a fake bomb under a table in the pub. The package was found by an off-duty soldier, at which bomb disposal experts were called and homes were evacuated. It took the experts until the early hours of the next day to establish that the package was a fake.

Police in Besançon, France, searched for four hours for the kidnappers of a thirteen-year-old boy before he admitted to having faked his own kidnapping to get out of going to school. The boy had forged his mother's signature on a letter explaining why he was late to school, but once he realised he had been found out he slashed his face with a knife and claimed he had been bundled into a car by some men.

Up in Flames

SETTING YOUR WORLD ON FIRE

Malcolm Foster, a fire-eater, was performing a medical skit at a New Zealand hospital as part of a fundraiser. Malcolm's stage name is Robbie Burns, and he certainly lived up to it when he blew out a ball of fire and sent his lacquered hairdo up in flames. Lucky he was in a hospital – though having said that the audience thought it was just part of the show and no one rushed to his aid.

A seventy-year-old patient at St Mary's Hospital, Portsmouth, ended up with a 'bush fire on his face' when he tried to sneak a cigarette. In order to get a good drag on his ciggie he had to remove his oxygen mask, and placing a lighted object near pure oxygen can only mean one thing – fire. It didn't help that the man had a luxuriant beard and moustache, which rapidly went up in flames. To add to the confusion, he reached under the bed with the cigarette to put it out of sight and set a bag on fire. In the ensuing blaze twenty firefighters were called to the ward and nineteen elderly patients had to be evacuated. The bearded firestarter was unharmed, if a little singed.

A goldfish bowl full of water was probably the cause of a fire that sent twenty-six people to hospital in Oxfordshire. Firefighters thought that a goldfish bowl in a shed in the back garden of a house acted to focus the sun's rays into another shed. The second shed contained rat-catcher's equipment, including various poisonous chemicals, which ignited and set the

burning issue STRANGE

We're not sure quite who's to blame here. The victim sued the hospital, so he clearly thought it was their fault; the hospital authorities, on the other hand, were satisfied that it was just a freak accident. Here's what happened at the Kjellerups hospital in Denmark:

A thirty-year-old man was having surgery to remove a mole on his on his backside. The operation was being carried out with an electric knife and the man's buttocks and genitals had been washed with surgical spirit, in keeping with normal hygienic procedure. In mid-operation, the patient broke wind, and a spark from the electric knife ignited the gas and set his alcohol-doused genitals alight. He woke up in excruciating pain down there, had to take extra time off work and was unable to have sex with his wife, hence the lawsuit for suffering and loss of income.

shed alight. When the fire brigade tried to dampen the blaze, the chemicals gave off such a noxious cloud of toxic fumes that eighteen firefighters, four paramedics and four neighbours were taken to hospital suffering from vomiting, nausea and burning chest pains. The goldfish did not survive the blaze.

You've heard of Moses and the burning bush. Well this story is about Paul and the exploding cactus. When Paul Henson from Peterborough, who has several cacti in a hot conservatory at his house, smelt smoke there, he assumed that his stepchildren had been playing with matches. He rushed in to find that a 10-inch-high cactus had just exploded and caught fire, sending up 18-inch flames, setting fire to other plants and melting part of his conservatory roof. Paul believes that cacti can explode in the wild, to spread their seeds, although a spokeswoman for the Royal Horticultural Society said: 'We have never heard of any plant spontaneously combusting, especially in the case of a cactus which lives in a desert.'

From burning bush to burning bushy eyebrows. Filming of a UK TV programme had to be stopped when one of the actors was set on fire. The reconstruction of the burning at the stake of a Protestant martyr stopped when the seventy-year-old actor, identified only as Bob, had to spend the night in Oxford's John Radcliffe Hospital after his voluminous eyebrows went up in flames. Rob Carey, the production director, says the fire was lit a short distance away from the actor but a swift gust of wind sent the flames in his direction.

In Papendrecht, Holland, a twenty-nine-year-old man who had got some nasty grease stains on a jumper had the bright idea of soaking it in petrol to get rid of the stains, before bunging it in the washing-machine. He overdid the petrol, though, and it reacted with the washing powder to cause an explosion that ripped through the roof and blew out some windows. The man was unhurt, but his jumper perished in the blast.

MONEY TO BURN

On a desperately busy night at Filthy McNasty's in Edinburgh, with cash flowing in as fast as the drink was flowing out, the barmaid, Eimar Kean, stashed £800 in the microwave for safekeeping since the till was overflowing. As she shut the door she unwittingly nudged the 'cook' switch. A few minutes later the bar was filled with the smell of burning, eventually traced to the microwave, where the £800 was ready, but no longer readies.

A group of robbers in Penrith, Australia, stole a cash machine from a service station by ramming it with their truck and dragging it out on a chain. During the speedy getaway, with the cash machine still on tow, friction caused by the heavy metal machine on the road and the speed of the truck began to generate heat. A lot of heat. Enough to cause the money inside the machine to catch fire. Doubtless swearing the air blue the thieves dumped their useless, smouldering haul and disappeared.

What is it about drinking establishments, cash and microwaves? A toddler set fire to £1,000 in notes after his mother put them in the microwave for safekeeping. Pub landlady Madeline Hill put the money she had been counting in the oven to answer a knock at the door. But in the few minutes she was away, twenty-month-old Jordan, who had seen his mother use the microwave many times, turned it on. 'He must have decided I had done it wrong and turned it on for me,' Madeline said. All that remained of the £1,000 were the metal strips at the bottom of the oven. Madeline was confident her insurance would cover the loss.

Beliefs

SUPERSTITIOUS NONSENSE

Villagers from Smulti in Galati, Romania, believe that while an oil painting of the Virgin Mary was being restored, the picture apparently repainted itself overnight. Restorer Gigel Dumitriu had removed some faded paint and planned to paint it back in the next day, only to find that it was already done. The villagers also claim that thieves once tried to steal the portrait but were unaccountably reduced to tears.

The University of Swansea, Wales, has an Egypt Centre which was visited by a woman who announced firmly that the death masks on display were possessed by spirits. She was told that, on the contrary, they had been made just a few weeks earlier by children from a local school.

There's no crime in the village of Simulia in India and for that reason none of the houses has a door (in fact, once, when a villager did install doors in his house, it went up in flames). Villagers believe that the local deity Kharakhai Devi protects them, and here's the proof, according to the village elder: once a boy from the next village went into an orchard and tried to steal some bananas. He became mysteriously confined in the orchard and was unable to return home, and, so the story goes, he had to be rescued the next day.

For most of us, choosing lottery numbers is, well, it's a lottery. In the northern Thai village of Ban Mae Keow, however, villagers have been flocking to see a pair of gold coloured eels caught by Kui Nuhchaipin in the Mae Keow river. He was planning to make a curry from them when his cousin stopped him and pointed out their incredible colour. The eels, clearly magical, were installed in a tank at his home and his neighbours believe they can predict lottery numbers. Dozens of residents now visit Mr Nuhchaipin's home to pray, light candles and offer incense and flowers to the eels – and, most importantly of course, to watch the movement of the eels for signs of the winning numbers

Some people will believe anything – including the fact that chartered accountants are boring. Not true if accountant Neil Burns, fifty-nine, of Kidderminster is anything to go by. With the help of a hypnotherapist, Neil has discovered that in past lives he has been an Inca mathematician and a schoolboy in Nazi Germany, as well as Anthony Babington, with whom Mary Queen of Scots had, according to the book Burns has now published, a rather salacious relationship. In one of the book's scenes Babington – that's Neil – encounters Mary wearing just her underwear and she commands him to birch her, which he willingly does. The book was reported to be selling well in Kidderminster.

nookie nightmares

Residents of Lautaro, a village in Chile, claim that their lives are being ruined by erotic nightmares. One woman, Olga Venegas, said she had been gripped by the nightmares for more than eight years, while her husband also reported being in need of a decent night's sleep. Sufferers said the wild erotic dreams usually begin some time after midnight and often last all night, and that the cause of it all is the fact that their district was built on the site of an old graveyard. The villagers claimed that demons possess them when they are asleep, causing the strange dreams, and exorcism was necessary to bring peace to their slumbers. Not all the locals have succumbed to the demonic dreams, and one sceptic called on his fellow residents to see a psychiatrist or a sex therapist.

It's amazing what people think will bring them bad luck. Like buying fruit and veg from a man who's had his penis amputated, for example. Manuel Aillapan, who lives on the Chilean island of Castro, had surgery on his penis which went wrong, with the result that his penis had to be amputated. It appears that the inhabitants of Castro are a superstitious lot at the best of times, believing that the island is controlled by wizards (definitely not the Chilean government then), and that there is a haunted ship cruising off the coast.

Consequently, no one would buy their greens from Manuel any more because they thought he would bring them bad luck. Manuel was unable to keep up the rent on his stall, which was repossessed, and he is facing bankruptcy.

Sadly, Beatle George Harrison died at the end of 2001. Just a few hours later, on the other side of the world, there was happiness as the Japanese royal couple announced the birth of their first baby. And this was no coincidence, according to reincarnation expert Dr Bruce Goldberg, who believes that the new baby is the reincarnation of George, who was a devout believer in reincarnation himself. Goldberg believes that George had the spiritual power to make it happen, but no one will know for sure whether the new Japanese royal is a Beatle for a few years yet.

A woman in China whose surname is 'Pei' has found that her name brings her very bad luck. She has been unable to find the employment she wants, in sales, because in Chinese her name sounds the same as a word that means 'lose money in business'. She is a university graduate, and has applied for dozens of jobs in her home city of Changchun, all with the same outcome – as soon as she tells potential employers her name, they lose interest.

A Greek civil servant refused to clock in at her office for four months and had her salary stopped as a result. When the case went to court it emerged that the woman wouldn't use the electronic clocking-in system because the microchip in her swipe card had the number 666 in it, and was clearly part of a satanist conspiracy. The State Legal Council consulted the software manufacturers, who denied any satanic link.

CURSES, CURSES

A Romanian dog owner hit upon an unusual way of getting his stolen dog, Rexi, back. Gheorghe Ferencz, of Sibiu, advertised in newspapers, invoking curses on the thief. Ferencz hoped the thief would never enjoy his dinner again, that he would never find peace, that he would go blind and that his teeth would fall out. In another curse he hoped the thief would crash his car into a tree. Return of the dog, or at least proof that Rexi was being well looked after, however, would mean that the curses would be lifted.

A century ago the villagers of Moudros on the Greek island of Limnos were put under a curse 'never to sleep again'. Monks in Mount Athos have been chanting the curse on the same day every year, 23 August, since Ottoman forces slaughtered almost all the monks on the island, believing the monks to have killed some of the occupying Ottoman troops. Two monks escaped the slaughter and, blaming the villagers for having brought about the murder of so many of their number, they laid the curse. A delegation of villagers recently came to the monastery and pleaded for the curse to be lifted, which is exactly what happened on 23 August. It wasn't revealed, though, whether the curse actually worked.

City Governor Samak Sundaravej of Bangkok put a curse on all the city's bins (worth about £20 each) to stop people stealing them. A curse was written on the bins warning people that they will suffer misfortune if they steal them. Mr Samak also put a curse on corrupt police officers shortly after he was elected – we don't know the upshot of that one.

In Luvvieland it is considered taboo to refer to Shakespeare's play *Macbeth* by name. Most thesps call it 'the Scottish play', the reason being that there is supposed to be a curse on it, and not just the curse of bad acting. Well ... according to recent attempts to remedy the situation, there could be something in it.

White witch Kevin Carlyon and psychic medium Eileen Webster tried to contact the spirit of King Macbeth of Scotland to exorcise the ancient curse, and were, according to their accounts, beset by strange happenings. They said that several other witches cancelled their trip to the site of the old Inverness Castle, in the Highlands of Scotland – one because of the 'unlucky' death of a pet dog and another because her cat brought in a black feather – and a cameraman ended up in hospital after falling ill while filming the ritual.

Mr Carlyon summoned the elements of earth, air, wind and water, while letting off industrial smoke bombs, and when Ms Webster attempted to contact Macbeth, she collapsed on the ground. She reported sensing 'a great power that just drained away all my energy. I remember feeling fear. I sensed a very, very evil spirit. I believe in this curse definitely now.' Ms Webster also said that she had been stalked by a black crow prior to the ceremony. Mr Carlyon summed the operation up by saying that they may have deflected the curse, but they wouldn't know until there was positive feedback from people putting on productions of the play.

WE WISH YOU A WEIRD CHRISTMAS

Christmas is a time of year that really brings out the weird in people …

Every now and then the UK's ubiquitous chip shops come up with a new (and stomach-churning) trend in battered, deep-fried convenience food. Glasgow, for example, became famous for the deep-fried Mars bar. Last Christmas, Ben Stylianou decided to give his customers at Benny's in Clapham, south London, the convenience of a full Christmas dinner battered and deep-fried. Benny's Christmas dinner fritters were filled with turkey, stuffing, potatoes, carrots, sprouts, peas and gravy – all for a mere £2.49. They proved to be a big hit with his regulars, and as the customers pointed out, they saved on the washing-up. Perfect.

A garden centre in Pennsylvania, USA, had a beautiful display involving two real reindeer, Donner and Blitzen. They both escaped, and Donner was quickly recaptured. Blitzen made it as far as a nearby forest, where a hunter promptly shot him, thinking he was a native deer. Police and the local wildlife commission both said they were not responsible since local hunting regulations don't cover reindeer.

The Braehead Shopping Centre in Glasgow, Scotland, announced in November that for the Christmas shopping period it would loan out temporary boyfriends to women who were either single or whose partners were, for some reason, not keen on joining them in the battle against the Christmas shopping hordes. The Shopping Boyfriend was, according to the organiser of the man-loan scheme, the ultimate retail therapist: enthusiastic, attentive, admiring and complimentary, to the extent of never failing to reassure her that, yes, her bum looks small in that dress.

too clever for the pot

A farmer in North Yorkshire trained a turkey to walk a tightrope and jump through a ring of fire. Colin Newlove of Low Marshes felt the bird's talents would be enough to save him from the dinner table at Christmas. He had also previously trained a horse to fetch sticks. He said that Trevor (the turkey) took to tightrope-walking brilliantly and had been requested to appear at shows. The eighteen-month-old turkey trained on his own farmyard tightrope, stretching out his wings to keep his balance. **WEIRD**

Vehicular Weirdness

HIT THE BRAKES!

Sometimes vehicles go where they're not supposed to, even though the people driving them ought to have some idea of where the brake pedal is.

A carload of nurses crashed through the wall of a house in Frosta, Norway, where a patient was waiting for them to visit. The nurses were about to turn into the man's driveway when their car was struck by a bus. The car was pushed right through the kitchen wall into the man's house, and although he suffered slight shock, he ended up administering treatment to the nurses, who had minor injuries.

This is taking driver courtesy to foolish extremes: a bus passenger was dropped at her front door after the bus she was riding on drove through her front wall and across her garden. Kathleen Privett was ready to get off the bus when it crashed instead of turning a corner in Hyde, Greater Manchester. The fifty-four-year-old ended up looking through the window of her home at her husband Alan.

A car salesman in Romsey started up a Peugeot 206 Cabriolet inside the showroom to show off its special sporty features to an interested customer who was indeed treated to a spectacular little show. The car shot forward, crashing through the showroom's glass doors and hitting a petrol station price sign outside the showroom. The £18,500 car was left with a badly dented bonnet, and the salesman with badly dented pride. He was still in a job at the end of the day, though, his boss said.

A nineteen-year-old from Worcestershire took advantage of his parents' absence on holiday to take his father's lovely Mercedes for a spin. Robert Drysdale's parents were forced to cut short their holiday in the Far East to return to their £300,000 Stourport home, where their son had somehow managed to crash the Mercedes CLK through the wall into the kitchen. The car was wedged several feet off the floor with its front end in the kitchen, and a fire service spokesman said that the car seemed to be keeping that part of the house up. Robert escaped unhurt.

In sensible, well-regulated British Columbia, Canada, drivers are required to retake their test every two years once they reach the age of eighty. And here's one very good reason why. An eighty-three-year-old man was trying to prove his roadworthiness when he got confused and stepped on the accelerator instead of the brake. His car shot backwards through the window at the test centre, ripping the door off another car as he passed it. The man's wife, waiting inside, had to be taken to hospital with chest pains brought on by the shock of it all. Police charged the man with unsafe driving. Oh, and he won't be getting his licence back either.

JOYRIDING

Stealing cars and whizzing around in them for an evening's entertainment is SO last millennium. This is the way to do it ...

A gang of young German tearaways, bored with riding round in the car they had stolen, broke into Gladbach airport in Möenchengladbach and succeeded in hotwiring the engine of a small plane. They even taxied it out on to the runway, but their moment of glory was dashed when the teenager at the controls stalled the engine. Realising that the game was up, the group, aged between six and sixteen, got back into their stolen car and sped off, with the police in hot pursuit. They smashed through the perimeter fence then continued their flight on foot. Three of the kids were arrested immediately, while the other three eluded capture.

Juniper Leisure, in Romsey, Hampshire, is an outdoor activity centre that has a working military tank on its grounds. The temptation was just too much for two men who managed to steal the tank and go on a joyride with a difference – whenever they crashed into something, they just rolled right over it and carried on. The 17.5-ton Abbot tank was driven into parked cars, through fences and over ploughed fields, followed by a police helicopter. After four-and-half hours, the thieves finally abandoned the vehicle in a field after smashing into a tree.

THIS IS YOUR CAPTAIN SPEAKING ... COULD YOU LEND ME SOME MONEY?

An airline captain had no choice but to organise a whip-round from his passengers to pay for the refuelling of their aircraft. The Air 2000 flight from London Gatwick to Malaga was diverted due to fog to Seville – but by the time the plane arrived Seville airport was closed. So on he flew to Faro, in Portugal, which by a freak of chance was also closed due to fog. With fuel supplies nearing exhaustion, the aircraft was obliged to land at Tangier in Morocco, where officials demanded immediate payment for the refuelling, and the pilot, whose credit card was at its limit, was forced to ask for funds over the intercom. The flight did eventually make it to Malaga.

Kendell Airlines in Australia isn't the biggest in the world, or even the biggest in Australia. So, when budget restrictions meant that professional catering had to be scrapped, pilots and flight attendants on the domestic service between Albury-Wodonga and Sydney offered passengers home made in-flight refreshments. Blueberry, chocolate, banana

and apple/cinnamon muffins were baked and served on the flights, and all six flight captains, four first officers and five flight attendants contributed in some way.

STOPPING AIRCRAFT WHEN YOU SHOULDN'T

It must have been an uneventful night in Albuquerque, New Mexico, USA, particularly for the police helicopter surveillance officer and civilian pilot who were carrying out night patrol duties. So at around 1 a.m. they decided to ease their nagging hunger pangs and landed the 'copter next to a Krispy Kreme doughnut store, dashed in, bought a dozen doughnuts, then flew back off into the night sky. The two now face disciplinary measures as well as the wrath of taxpayers, who feel that at a cost of $80 an hour to maintain, a police helicopter used for a doughnut run is not a good thing.

The pilot of a private light aircraft could not hold out any longer. He'd already landed at Calgary International, and, with his bladder at bursting point, drove his Cessna on to the grass beside the runway. Unfortunately, this alerted the emergency services and the man relieved himself as the fire and ambulance crews roared up to him. Police released him without charge since officials couldn't see that he'd broken any regulations.

Two men were charged by Florida, USA, police after landing their helicopter on a public beach because they needed to go to the toilet. The two, Jacques Aube and Joseph Guy Lajoie, were en route from Canada to Fort Lauderdale in Florida when they were caught short, and landed on Flagler Beach. Locals thought they had come down for a spot of lunch; the police were less amused and booked them.

ANIMAL ENIGMAS

There is a science called cryptozoology which is the study of animals that might exist, ranging from the improbables, like the Loch Ness Monster, through the possibles, like Bigfoot/yeti/sasquatch, to the probables, such as animals which were thought to be extinct but are not. Every year or so a new species turns up, too. And every year there are sightings of the old regulars and new additions to the vast databank of stories about them.

Scientists in Australia discovered that a mysterious purple wallaby, thought to be a legend, does actually exist. A biologist named Le Souf claimed to have discovered the species in 1924, but his claims were ignored. The main reason for the rejection of his theory was that the pigment that causes the purple colouring fades when the animal dies, so by the time Le Souf had brought a creature back from its native area in north Queensland for inspection in Brisbane or Sydney, the wallaby looked like a normal rock wallaby, and his insistence that it had indeed had a purple-coloured face and neck was met with disbelief. Now, using new genetic techniques, researchers have confirmed that the purple-necked rock wallaby is indeed an entirely new species, although they do not yet know how the purple pigment is produced.

There are regions of the world where yeti stories are common, the best known being the Himalayas. Bigfoot country is clearly the densely wooded, mountainous region of America's Pacific Northwest. Here's a new report from an area that isn't so well known as yeti habitat. A frontier guard in the mountainous Aktalinsky district of the republic of Kyrgyzstan found the gigantic footprints of a mysterious humanoid creature. The length of a footprint was 45 centimetres, and its width 30 centimetres, so the creature was clearly of massive stature. The footprints, which were fairly fresh when the guard found them, were very clearly set in the clay soil of a riverbank. Experts said sightings had been made twenty years earlier in the neighbouring Pamir mountains, and theorised that military activity in that region could have caused the creature to migrate to Kyrgyzstan.

A rumour has been circulating among scientists and cryptozoologists in the USA – and we must stress that this is a rumour – that a scientist caught live footage of a Bigfoot by accident. According to a report, a scientist was conducting an environmental study in the vicinity of the upper Feather River Canyon in California. This involved taking photographs and video using cameras with night vision, a strategy commonly employed when researching environmental documents either to archive nocturnal wildlife species in areas prior to logging operations or to document the presence of endangered species.

The story goes that the scientist had baited a site with an animal carcass, then staked out the site, watching with night-vision technology. When he detected movement, he started filming. As he watched through the camera lens, he supposedly saw and filmed a Bigfoot inspecting the baited site. After a month, he reportedly destroyed the tape, fearing his career would be ruined if he went public.

A hunter in the northern wilds of Canada's Yukon territory got the surprise of his life when the bull moose he shot turned out to be neither male nor female. It was both. Rick Ward, a moose biologist for the Yukon government said that it was a hermaphrodite moose – a female with antlers – and added that he had never seen anything like it in all his twenty-five years as a biologist (fifteen of which have been spent studying moose). The vast Yukon territory, lying next to Alaska, is home to about 60,000 moose. Hunting of male moose is permitted for three months in the autumn of every year, and those who shoot one can live on its meat for a winter. But hunters who shoot cows face steep fines. Ward said the hunter, who called wildlife authorities after discovering the incredibly rare quirk of nature, was not fined.

PARANORMAL INSURANCE

Ultraviolet, a UK insurance company have set up a Spooksafe policy, to cover the costs of an attack by a ghost or poltergeist, a close encounter of the third kind (that's with aliens) or transformation into a werewolf or vampire. The Bristol-based group said that since the policy was launched there had been massive take-up and it wrote around 500 policies, mainly in California. Now you're probably thinking that they'd never pay out, but Ultraviolet coughed up the full £100,000 on one of the policies for a woman who died after being thrown over the banisters. A team of investigators concluded that a ghost was responsible, and Simon Burgess, chief underwriting officer, was satisfied with their findings.

Ultraviolet's policy will pay out £1 million to anyone who can medically prove that they have been transformed into a vampire or werewolf. Mr Burgess says the werewolf policy was extremely popular, with around a thousand people taking out cover in the year; dozens of vampire policies were also sold.

GHOSTLY GOINGS-ON

After seven years of troublesome happenings in their house, a couple in Norman, Oklahoma, USA, decided to ask the ghost responsible what the problem was. Jon and Agi Lurtz's house had been haunted since 1994 by the ghost of a University of Oklahoma physics professor, who, among other things, caused light bulbs to pop and even cranked up the stereo to the German metal

phantom panty droppers

The owners of Pillow Talk, a sex shop in Margate, Kent, believe that their premises are haunted. And not just by any old ghosts. By coincidence (we assume) their store is on the site of an old brothel, and it is the ex-employees who have come back to create a nuisance. Staff at Pillow Talk arrive most mornings to find bras and knickers thrown on the floor, French maids' outfits lying over the back of chairs and hanging from door handles and a general state of chaos. Owner Alan Butler said that only he and the manager have keys to the shop, so it isn't the work of pranksters, and he was convinced that something very strange was going on.

band Rammstein. Agi, who said she had often lived in haunted houses and could speak to the spirits, asked professor Sybrand Broersma why he was still around making mischief, and his reply was that he'd never had an obituary when he died back in 1987. So Jon and Agi duly ran an obituary in the local paper and their house is now a haven of ghost-free peace and quiet.

HOW DID YOU KNOW THAT?

Dreams that come true ...

A man who dreamed he would find buried treasure in his garden, in the south of England, spent thousands of pounds digging it up. There was absolutely no

life-saving premonition ODD

Roger Bousquet woke with a jolt at 2 a.m. in Houston, USA, totally convinced that something was wrong at home, 1,200 miles away in South Bend, Indiana. He rang his wife, Cheryl, but there was no answer, so he rang his in-laws, who immediately went over to the house, where Cheryl and their nine-year-old twin daughters were discovered unconscious from carbon monoxide poisoning. They all recovered safely, thanks to Roger's sudden awakening.

sign of any pirate gold or ancient coins, but the excavation opened up a well of mineral-rich water that is very likely to make him a fortune.

Harry Maertens, from Winnipeg in Canada, often dreamed that he'd have a big lottery win before he turned forty. With one month to go before hitting the big four-O, Harry had his most vivid dream yet. When he woke up he felt the money was already his, so strong was the feeling his dream had given him. So he went out and bought several lottery tickets at a variety of locations, among them eight scratch cards. The fifth of these cards had the big prize: 1 million dollars.

WEIRD WEATHER

If you want to get rid of ice and snow, just scatter sand on it. But holidaymakers at swish Alpine ski resorts like Zermatt and Verbier certainly did not want their lovely snow covered in the 80,000 tonnes of Saharan sand that fell from the sky, turning their glorious, gleaming white slopes brown, and bringing an early end to the ski season. Rising water vapour had sucked sand from Algeria and Morocco into huge clouds, then an atmospheric depression carried it across the Mediterranean and up the Rhone valley. When the sand-bearing clouds reached Lake Geneva their path was blocked by a cold front and they began to dump their load, turning white snow brown and chasing away thousands of disappointed skiers. It's an ill wind that blows nobody any good, though, as Geneva's car washes were reported to be doing a roaring trade throughout the weekend.

A shower of corn husks rained down on Wichita, Kansas. One local resident, whose name, spookily, happened to be Mr Corn, estimated the number of falling husks to be around a thousand, while a meteorologist declared that corn husks falling from the sky was 'odd' (you don't say – you learnt that in meteorology college?), pointing out also that not only were there no tornadoes, but it wasn't even particularly windy that day.

The colours of the rainbow are usually seen in the sky, not in the rain itself. But in the south Indian state of Kerala rain fell that was red, yellow, green and black. Scientists reckoned that the multicoloured precipitation was the result of meteor dust in the atmosphere, and reports from the Centre for Earth Sciences in Thiruvanthapuram of a burning meteor seemed to bear out this theory.

Pranks & Practial Jokes

GOTCHA!

Practical jokes are usually only funny for the perpetrators, never the victims. But they can be funny for the readers …

An early-morning jogger on a Florida beach came across a mound of sand with a sign on it saying that there was a baby buried there. Frank Cook, of Jupiter, immediately contacted police, who quickly arrived and set about uncovering what was buried there. Two feet down they dug up a box. Carefully, they opened the box and a furious skunk leapt out, spraying everyone within range before running off.

A twenty-two-year-old Norwegian woman was on a ferry crossing from Denmark to Norway when she was invited to take part in a game organised by fellow passengers. They challenged her to swap her clothing with another woman on stage while wearing a black plastic rubbish bag and blindfolded. Once the blindfold was firmly in place, they swapped the black bin liner for a transparent one, and she appeared naked in front of a crowd of hundreds. This was a joke that turned very sour for the middle-aged men who organised it, since the woman was angry enough to sue them and she won £1,300 in damages from them.

A honeymooning couple from Plymouth returned home to find that some wag had bricked up their front door and then painted a new one on to the bricks.

Forty-four-year-old Jeffrey Barber, of Pennsylvania, USA, fired a rifle in his house then daubed himself with tomato ketchup, and lay on the floor, hoping to give his wife a fright. She did indeed get a fright and immediately went and called the emergency services. The policeman who arrived promptly arrested Barber for illegally possessing the .22 calibre rifle (Barber was not allowed to own a gun because he had previous firearms offences), and he was given a fifteen-year sentence.

GNOME AND AWAY

Harmless little garden decorations or an assault on good taste that must be done away with? Or maybe even little individuals that shouldn't be kept in the confines of people's gardens but allowed to roam the earth as free as they day they were born? Whatever, there's a distinct trend for garden gnomes and their brethren to be liberated, much to the distress of their owners.

Ken and Olive Brockman of Buxton Road, Chingford, suffered the heartbreak of having their garden gnome, Nobby, kidnapped. And in a tortuous

twist designed to tug on their heartstrings they have been receiving postcards from the gnome as its abductors travel the country. From Cornwall he wrote of his taste for Cornish pasties, and cards also arrived at the Brockman's home from Norfolk, Dublin and Bournemouth. At least they know he's still safe and well.

What happens in Chingford can happen in Canada ... Tara and Keith Zalischuk of Calgary had a similar story to tell. When the most recent addition to their family of garden gnomes disappeared one day, they thought it strange and a bit unlikely that thieves would steal only one gnome when there were four at their mercy. And sure enough, it turned out to be the work of kidnappers, not thieves. Weeks later, the gnome was found back in his flower patch, for all the world as if nothing had happened. Except that on the Zalischuk's front doorstep there was a photograph album containing pictures of the gnome in London, in Paris, in Amsterdam … and also at a wedding in Saskatchewan. They were able to verify that it was their gnome in the photos thanks to a chip on his forehead. Along with the photos were two letters, one a history of his gnome heritage, the other an apology for his abrupt departure.

French activists committed to freeing garden gnomes struck in Rosheim, in the Alsace region. They removed fifteen gnomes from gardens and their owners later suffered the shock of being informed by the police that their gnomes had been found hanging from trees. These atrocities were carried out by the French Liberation Front of Garden Gnomes, who had on an earlier occasion left hundreds of liberated gnomes on a football pitch in Les Deux-Sevres.

Pinky and Perky are companion pigs in the garden of Moira Briggs of Kesgrave, Suffolk – or at least they were until Pinky was stolen. The 18-inch stone pig appears to have been travelling the world since then, as Moira has received letters and postcards from UK locations as well as from New York. One of the letters said that Pinky would be back after he had done a bit of travelling.

Food & Drink

FOOD FIGHTS BACK

The heat gets too much and the food can't take it any more. It snaps, it loses control and then it seeks its revenge …

It was a busy night in a restaurant in Athens, Greece. Suddenly, into the crowds of diners flew a lamb chop, shot like a bullet from an exploding oven. It struck George Kafatos, killing him, and hurt five other diners.

In the north German town of Uslar, a stall selling takeaway sausages exploded, shattering windows and showering the area with hot cooked meat. One man suffered concussion.

A fire destroyed sixty-two houses in a village in central Cambodia, leaving about 400 people homeless. The blaze started when a roasted cat caught fire, with the flames passing easily from shack to shack through the village. The cat-roasting fire-starter was a young man who enjoyed a bit of roast cat and few glasses of wine with his friends.

DON'T EAT THAT! YOU DON'T KNOW WHERE IT'S BEEN

What tipped a woman from Aberdeen off that there may have been something slightly amiss with her dog was the strange crunching noise she heard whenever she stroked it. A visit to the vet revealed that the pooch had been eating more than just dog food and had thirty-two pebbles in its belly.

A woman in Shibata, Japan, bought a custard pudding and took it home. When it was opened, the pudding was found to have an extra ingredient – a small frog.

A Colorado shop worker drank two-thirds of a bottle of Ora Potency (honest!) Fruit Punch before discovering that there was a severed penis in it. A pathologist conformed it was a penis, but it was not known whether it came from an adult or a child.

WEIRD

condom curry

Emily Lewis-Shepherd of Cardiff, Wales, bought a ready-made chicken curry from her local supermarket. As she was giving it a stir before tucking into it for her lunch she noticed an odd-looking tomato skin, so she pulled it out. And it wasn't a tomato skin at all. It was a strawberry-flavoured condom. It even still smelled of strawberries.

Mysteriously, the seal was not broken when Juan Sanchez-Marchez bought the drink, and at the bottling plant it was stated that there was no way a penis could have got into a bottle. Further tests revealed that the object was not, in fact, a penis, but a very lifelike chunk of penis-shaped mould. It emerged that the pathologist had not taken tissue samples from the mystery object, since a visual check had appeared to confirm its identity.

It's hard in the Russian army, damned hard. And some soldiers go above and beyond the call of duty when it comes to trying to get out. Like the frontier guard in the Primorye region who ate half his bed. As the nineteen-year-old's health deteriorated, a surgeon operated and found and removed more than forty pieces of the man's army bunk from his stomach. And since the operation was done with the soldier fully conscious, he was able to tell the surgeon after each removal how many more bits were likely to be in there.

lizard lunch

Mr Amresh Singh, of Lucknow, India, confessed to a special way of getting high: he eats lizards. About five or six will apparently provide him with enough of the mildly poisonous flesh to give him the rush he needs. Once he's consumed the lizards there's the small matter of losing consciousness, bleeding from his orifices and having breathing difficulties. But obviously it's worth it.

BIZARRE

nicotine nibbles

A sixty-one-year-old woman in southern India has a cigarette addiction – but it's the stubs she can't do without, and she eats them rather than smoking them. Khayarunnisa, from Kotamedu in Tamil Nadu state, collects and eats the stubs of India's traditional cigarette, the beedi, in which tobacco is rolled into a leaf and tied with a cotton thread. Every morning she begins her scavenge of the streets, picking up the beedi stubs before the street cleaners get to them. She started fifty years ago (her father was a heavy smoker, and she used to eat his discarded fag-ends) and cannot now contemplate a life without them. In fact, Khayarunnisa said that she lost her taste for normal food a long time ago, and has the advantage of not having to worry about cooking for herself – plus her food is free.

Athletes tend to take nutrition seriously, sometimes searching out unusual foodstuffs in their effort to stay fitter than the rest. When Australian Jacqui Cooper fractured a vertebra – an injury which threatened to put her out of the Winter Olympics at Salt Lake City, where she was hoping to compete in aerial freestyle skiing – she took crushed cockroaches in diet Coke to recover. Apparently it's fairly hard on your stomach, but it does speed up recovery from injuries.

When a woman ordered a vanilla cream cake at a café in Rome and bit into it she got a mouthful of bat. It seems that the bat had been hanging around the roof of the bakery and had fallen on to the production line.

An easy mistake to make: a couple from Bewdley, Worcestershire, suffered severe food poisoning when they prepared a meal incorporating daffodil bulbs, which they had mistaken for onions.

Ethiopian Gezahenge Debebe, forty, complained of stomach pains, and x-rays revealed that his stomach was stuffed with various pieces of metal. Surgeons spent over an hour extracting keys, coins and 222 rusty nails. It was thought that Gezahenge had been eating metal on the quiet for around twenty years.

DRUNK AGAIN ...

Booze does funny things to your brain, including making you forget that very fact after a few drinks, with the result that you carry on drinking. The results can be weird.

Michael McMillian was on the stand, accused of drunk driving, the arresting officer having claimed that his eyes were 'glassy'. Ah, but the reason for this, responded the defendant's lawyer, reaching over to McMillan's face and removing his glass eye, was, indeed, his glass eye. The judge found him guilty anyway, ruling that the other eye was glassy too.

Gary Carter, a printer from Trimdon, Durham, had a bit of a drink – an all-day session, in fact, and he was spotted the next day asleep in the branches of a sycamore tree, 25 feet above the ground. No one knows how he got up there, least of all Gary, since the trunk of the tree is bare most of the way up. The County Durham Fire Brigade was called, and, to the firemen's astonishment, Gary remained far away in the land of nod for the entire two-hour rescue operation. Gary's only memory of the whole episode is waking up in hospital, where he was taken for health checks.

A forty-nine-year-old man was stopped by police in Moenchengladbach, Germany, when they noticed the rather erratic progress of the electric wheelchair in which he was riding. Showing great resourcefulness, the man had borrowed his father's buggy to go out and buy a drop more to drink because he had already consumed so much that he was incapable of walking.

Bears like a drop too. Potapych was bought as a cub by a successful Russian businessman to impress his friends, and when his owner was sent to jail, he was cared for by Uncle Misha. Since Misha was an alcoholic, Potapych quickly got used to being offered a drop by Misha, and it wasn't long before they would spend evenings getting drunk together. Eventually Potapych was identified as a threat, as his drunken moods weren't pretty, and he was taken away to the state zoo – completely drunk, since Misha had organised one last boozy binge the night before.

WEIRD

hello darlin'

A thirty-three-year-old Norwegian man who went to a party at the house of his ex-partner's parents proceeded to get so drunk there that when he left, intending to visit his ex-, he went into the wrong bedroom of the wrong house, stripped off and got into bed with the wrong woman, whom he began to fondle. She woke up at this point and made him aware of his error. Although he ended up in court, Trondheim magistrates believed that it was an honest mistake and acquitted him of charges of housebreaking and sexual assault. The woman did look a bit like his ex- too.

Fuelled with much alcohol, and the arrogance of (relative) youth, a thirty-eight-year-old man accepted a challenge from a fifty-year-old that if he, the younger man, could outswim him in San Fransisco Bay, the older man would give him his car. The younger man never got the car, because he drowned.

A drunken joke turned into a nightmare when a Canadian man was charged with having sex with a cat. The thirty-nine-year-old told the court in Toronto that after he and his boyfriend had showered, having spent a whole day on the booze, they posed some rude-looking shots featuring the man and the cat, for a laugh of course, and later sent them to the chemist's to be developed. That, of course, is how they were found out, but a subsequent examination of the cat by a vet showed that she had not been interfered with.

A twenty-two-year-old partygoer from Chemnitz in Germany had been taken to hospital having been found unconscious from alcohol poisoning. He came round in hospital, at least enough to realise that he had been taken away from the party and the booze, and his instinctive reaction was to go to the ambulance bay and steal an ambulance which he managed to drive back to the party and hide in the garden before rejoining the festivities. Some other partygoers, doubtless jealous of his clearly superhuman powers, rang the police to complain about the ambulance and he was nicked.

A cocktail dubbed the 'atomic cocktail' did for a twenty-seven-year-old Chilean man on his stag night, to the extent that he slipped into a coma after drinking it. His lamentably drunken state meant that his wedding day went by the board as well, since he had to remain under medical attention for another three weeks. What was the subtle blend of ingredients that made this cocktail so effective? It was a mix of spirits, mustard, margarine and bacon, drunk with the utmost delicacy from a washing-up bowl.

Linda Harris was arrested for drunk driving in Las Cruces, New Mexico, USA, after work colleagues saw her parking erratically when she turned up at a special picnic. She failed four out the five sobriety tests. Ironically, the picnic was for an alcohol awareness day, and Linda's job was co-ordinator of an anti-drink-driving programme in Las Cruces.

Looks, Looks, Looks

HAIRCUT, SIR?

A barber had to be flown all the way from Scotland at government expense to the Netherlands, just to cut the hair of accused Pan Am Flight 103 bomber – and Scottish prisoner – Abdel Basset al-Megrahi, because security policy prevented local civilians from doing it.

You have to be careful how you treat the man who's cutting your hair. Take the case of the man in the Mauritanian capital of Nouakchott who asked his barber to redo his hair over and over again. The young stylist was desperate to leave work on time because he had a hot date, but this customer kept telling him to make a change here and a change there. In a fit of exasperation the barber, named as Ahmadu, sliced off part of the customer's ear. Police ruled the contest a draw.

Lord Jeffrey Archer, though once a leading figure in the Conservative party, is possibly more famous for being a best-selling novelist, and for his lying, cheating past which finally caught up with him when he was jailed for perjury in 2001. During his last haircut as a free man, the flamboyant millionaire peer's hairdresser, Daniel Hersheson, whose clients include superstars such as Jennifer Aniston and Elle Macpherson, was overheard to tell his jail-bound client that he would still do his hair even if he was sent down. The bad news for Lord Archer though was that UK prison regulations forbid inmates to be seen by their personal stylists, and fellow convicts volunteer for hair-cutting duty.

QUIRKY COUTURE

Ioana Cioanca, of Bistrita, Romania, will be wearing a new raincoat for the winter season, over a matching blouse and skirt, along with a hat, shawl, handbag and even a purse – all of which she has crocheted herself. All the items are in the same shade of brown, and have been made with fallen strands of Ioana's hair which she has been collecting since she was seventeen. She's now sixty-four. Ioana started collecting her hair when her grandmother told her it was a sin to throw it away. She never uses shampoo because she says it poisons the hair, and only ever washes it with home-made soap and rainwater. Ioana wears her hair outfits for best – to church, for example. Maybe she has a family hair loom.

Claudia Escobar is a Chilean fashion designer, and she came up with a bikini that's more suited to the water than any other – it's made from salmon skin. Claudia's always wanted to explore more exotic materials and says she's always been a fish fan. Even though salmon skins are cheap to get hold of – usually producers of tinned salmon just throw them away – Claudia intends to charge top dollar for her scaly sunwear. 'Hermès charge $7,000 for an ostrich skin wallet', said Claudia, adding that this price gave her something to aim at. We don't know if you'll swim faster in a salmon skin bikini, but you may be the only one on the beach with one. If you can afford it.

CHEATING BEAUTY QUEENS

The things people will do for a paltry fifteen minutes of fame. A contestant for Miss France was disqualified after having her spine stretched in order to appear taller. Aurélie Brun was beautiful enough – but not tall enough to meet the 1.72 metres minimum height requirement, so she had the operation to gain an extra 3.8 centimetres. It worked, and she won the Miss Loire-Forez title and entered the rounds for the Miss France contest. A competitor guessed her secret though and told organisers, who disqualified her. It didn't matter, though, because Aurélie had shrunk back to her normal height and wouldn't have been eligible anyway.

To show how easy it was to win a beauty contest, a journalist from the Spanish newspaper El Mundo entered a regional contest – Miss Alicante – and bribed a judge. Gema Garcia Marcos, thirty-one, won the Miss Alicante crown after she offered 27,000 euros to a judge, despite being seven years too old for the contest and barely able to walk in high heels. The bribery transaction, filmed by a hidden camera and shown in a television documentary, would have put Garcia Marcos in line for the Miss Spain contest, but she was disqualified when her age was discovered.

Another dip into the murky pool of vanity: Jannette Velazquez won the Miss Puerto Rican Queen Pageant at a festival in New Jersey, but organisers were later obliged to disqualify her since the fifteen-year-old girl had claimed to be sixteen on her application form. Jannette and her mother clearly felt that she was still the most beautiful in the contest though and hung on to the crown and other prizes so that the pageant officials ended up charging them with theft.

LIFE'S LITTLE IRONIES

Chris Axworthy, justice minister for Saskatchewan, Canada, left his home to announce a government crackdown on car thieves. He had to get a lift to the press conference from a colleague, though, because his car had been stolen.

This year's Swim for Boston Harbor, held each summer at South Boston's M Street Beach to celebrate the recent clean-up of Boston's beaches and the pure water now there to swim in, was cancelled. Heavy rain caused the city's sewage system to overflow, flooding the bay with raw human waste.

After attending their conference on food poisoning, held at the Public Health Laboratory Service in Colindale, London thirty of the seventy-eight delegates went down with the campylobacter bug, probably contracted from their lunch.

The opening of a hotel owned by America's national plumbers' and pipe fitters' union was delayed by a burst water pipe. Conference rooms on the second and third floors at the United Association's Florida hotel were drenched, causing a three-week delay to the launch.

A secondary school in Lothian, Scotland, put together an anti-drugs play. The play had unfortunately, however, to be cancelled when it was discovered that two of the cast members had been smoking cannabis.

Police organised an anti-drugs talk at Ilfracombe Community College, Devon, to which, as they always do, they brought along a sniffer dog. The dog did not know, however, that it wasn't on duty, and sniffed out a stash of cannabis. Four boys were arrested.

As Governor Rangarajan warmed to his speech to the parliament of the Indian state of Andhra Pradesh, a speech that would highlight improvements to the power supply ... you've guessed it – a power cut plunged the parliament into darkness. The power supply failed again later, just as the opposition leader was holding a press conference in an adjoining room.

A Dutch couple on holiday in Turkey made friends with an adorable little stray kitten. Freddie Joling

video nasty

IRONIC

To help prepare a sixty-three-year-old woman in Workington for open heart surgery she was shown a helpful video demonstrating the op she was about to undergo. But guess what? She got scared and had a heart attack.

and Ellie Boer loved it so much that when they heard that the authorities were planning to cull all stray cats, they spent hundreds of pounds to fly back out to Bodrum, rescue Shansle, as they had named the cat, and take it back home to Holland. Shansle didn't adapt too well to the busier traffic conditions in her new home though, and before long she was run over by a car and killed.

A group of very drunk hunters cut off electric power to a third of the population of Kyrgyzstan's capital Bishkek when they used ceramic insulators on high-voltage lines for target practice. One building that suffered the thirty-minute blackout on Friday was a hotel hosting a conference on alcohol abuse. Delegates, including Deputy Prime Minister Nikolai Tanayev, were obliged to take a coffee break.

Now the thing about feng shui is that an expert comes to your house, instructs you to make changes in it according to the principles of feng shui, and then you just sit back and wait for your life to change.

This is exactly what happened to Annette and Tony Radley of Ross-on-Wye, but not in quite the way you might imagine. Annette Radley, forty-four paid £300 to an expert from a London firm specialising in the ancient Chinese art.

The expert ordered her to move son, Christopher, seventeen, from his bedroom into the snooker room of their five-bedroom, £300,000 house. She told Annette to paint butterflies on wooden beams, to change the position of mirrors in every room, to stick bamboo flutes to the ceiling and re-arrange garden ornaments. She also insisted that putting crystals in a bowl was essential. Soon after the consultation, Annette's family was hit by a string of disasters. Her husband Tony lost his £150,000 a year job as managing director of a refrigeration company; Annette crashed her car four times, although she was not badly injured; and within days of the expert's visit husband and wife were rowing incessantly, despite over twenty years of happy marriage. In fact, they ended up getting divorced. Annette said later that she had trusted the woman from the feng shui company, but in fact the 'expert' had only read one book on the subject.

When Italian priest Giuseppe Pierantoni was kidnapped in the Philippines by armed men who held him to ransom somewhere in the jungles of the Lanao del Sur region, police brought in a specially trained kidnap negotiator, providing him with the ransom money (the equivalent of around £48,500). The next thing they heard, Father Giuseppe was still in the jungle and the negotiator had run off with the money. Perhaps the kidnappers got wind of the fact that the money had disappeared, because they eventually released the priest.

Les Price is big – 25 stone (159 kilograms) to be precise. And when he flew from his native Wales to Ireland to support the Welsh rugby team, he was desperately uncomfortable squashed into the unforgiving little plane seat. So for the return flight he decided to splash out and he booked two seats together, so he could stretch out and get comfortable. You can imagine then how annoyed he was to find that he had indeed been given two seats with consecutive numbers; but on opposite sides of the aisle.

GET YOUR KICKS

A thirty-seven-year-old Italian man admitted to having robbed twenty-one banks because he was looking for kicks after his wife dumped him. The man, from Torino, was arrested after robbing two banks within forty minutes with a toy gun on his way home from work. He told police, in front of a judge, that he had undertaken the robberies to help him cope with his depression. After each robbery he hid outside to watch the police turn up, which, as he said, gave him a 'thrill comparable to being with a woman'.

A young Australian mother says she streaked in front of 20,000 rugby league fans wearing just a pair of sunglasses and a pair of big foam hands to 'feel alive again'. Catherine Maher, twenty-eight, was given forty hours of community service after pleading guilty at Brisbane magistrates court. She ran the full length of the pitch naked at the Brisbane Broncos' ground, and after her streak she danced under the goal posts before police and security guards escorted her away. Maher had left her children with a babysitter because she was expecting to be arrested.

THE STRENGTH OF TEN

You hear stories about people being given other-wordly strength by – what, we don't quite know. Adrenaline, maybe, or divine intervention if you like. But either way, such events do occur …

An Australian tree lopper in Melbourne who had the misfortune to have an 800-kilogram (that's nearly a ton) tree fall on him was freed by his workmate, who drew on superhuman powers and somehow managed to lift the tree off his mate's legs before the ambulance services arrived.

Richard Stilwell, of Bow, New Hampshire, USA, was working under his van when it rolled down a ramp and ended up on top of him. The full-size Dodge Ram van weighed about 1,818 kilograms, and Richard was totally and utterly trapped beneath it. That's when Superwoman flew in. At 5 feet 2 inches and weighing just 50 kilograms, Richard's wife Donna is no body-builder, but she managed to lift up the van (which was thirty-six times her own body weight) so that Richard could crawl to safety. She attempted a repeat perform-ance later, but could not lift the van more than a centimetre off the ground

WEIRD IS BLIND

A woman in Reading, England, called the RSPCA inspectors to say she had located a rare baby owl.

ODD

i see his his logic

A Swedish man appealed to his country's television authority for a half-price TV licence because he is blind in one eye and partially sighted in the other. The request was refused.

When they arrived they discovered a rather grubby bath sponge being held protectively by an extremely short-sighted woman.

Ramzan Ali, a barber in New Delhi, India, once cut a customer's hair with his eyes shut to prove his mastery of the craft. And that's what got him to thinking … why not set up a school for blind barbers? His class of ten boys in New Delhi were nervous about cutting customers' ears instead of their hair at first but now they're more confident. Of course, when you go to a barber's what you want most of all is to walk away with your ears intact – it doesn't matter what the hair-cut looks like, does it?

A Brazilian football team, Madureira, has hired a trainer who is almost completely blind. Former footballer Anísio Cabral de Lima, sixty-four, lost most of his sight during a game when he was hit in the face by a ball. And when the game has given you so much, you've got to try to give something back, haven't you? De Lima says he can see the shape of players and knows what's happening from the crowd's reaction.

Club president Ivan Tenorio also pointed out that one of the team's players is responsible for describing to de Lima what's happening on the field.

Amy, a Dobermann, is a guide dog for the blind. Slightly unusual in as much as Dobernmanns are not often used as guide dogs. But it's when you find out who she is a guide for that it really gets weird. Amy is a guide for Emma, another Dobermann. She lives with Elaine Dowd and Lisa Gustafson in Ottawa, Canada, wears a bell on her collar and enables Emma to go shopping, swimming, avoid running into the furniture and so on.

WHAT'S IN A NAME?

A rose by any other name, they say ... Not everyone agrees with that sentiment, though. Here are some examples:

A street in Bundaleer Forest, in South Australia's remote outback, was named after a local councillor. Nothing unusual in that, except that it was given his nickname: Turd. Protests from residents that the road sign was sending out the wrong message to tourists were heard and the Turd Terrace sign was duly removed.

The village of Doulting, in Somerset, has many lovely houses. One, where Chris Atyeo lives, was named by him Fuque Hall, as a joke. But the irony was lost on a company called Décor Art who featured the house on a range of six limited-edition plates edged with 18-carat gold.

In the Peak District in Derbyshire there are many interesting caves to visit. The Peak Cavern is one of them, but visitor numbers were less than satisfactory until the management decided to revert to the cavern's original Anglo-Saxon name, given because of the farting noise made by water draining out of the cavern. The Devil's Arse, as it is now called, attracts 30 per cent more visitors than it did before.

Back to Australia again, where a fifty-six-year-old man from the state of Victoria waged a legal battle to keep his adopted name. He took the name 'Prime Minister John Piss the Family Court and Legal Aid' in 1997, and is known as John for short. He already uses the name on his driving licence, bank account and medical records, but came up against a brick wall when he tried to get a passport in that name

– the passport office weren't happy about putting John's full name on a passport. The dispute reached Australia's Federal Magistrates Court, where the passport office's lawyer contended that the name was 'insulting and contemptuous of the Family Court'.

In the densely wooded region of north-western Maine, USA, there have been a few changes to local place names. Actually, several names, but only one change. So what's been going on? A new state law decreed that any names with the word 'squaw' in them had to be changed, because that word, originally referring to women's genitals (funny, no one seems to object to Beaver Creek), was offensive to Native Americans. Officials registered their dissatisfaction with the enforced change by substituting the word 'moose', where once 'squaw' had been used. With five different places already called Moose Pond, as well as a Moose Cove, Moose Island, several Moose Creeks and a village called Moosehead, all on the shores of Moosehead Lake, this change added considerably to the number of Moose names in the region. Now visitors to the area will stare bemusedly at a map that also contains Moose Bay, Moose Brook, Little Moose Brook, Little Moose Pond, Big Moose Pond, Big Moose Mountain, Little Moose Township, Moose Point and a mountain officially known as Moose Bosom. Similar legislation in Minnesota took years to enact because objecting local authorities tried to replace Squaw Creek and Squaw Bay with the names Politically Correct Creek and Politically Correct Bay.

According to analysts of US census and Social Security Administration records, the list of children's names gets stranger and stranger with every year that passes. The last complete year for which full records are available is 2000, and recently released reports show that alongside the two commonest boys' and girls' names, Jacob and Emily, were boys named Ventura (as in Jesse Ventura, WWF star), Timberland, Canon (as in the camera manufacturer) and Blue; while there were girls named Vanity, Whisper, Sincere and Unique. It goes on: there were boys named Truth and girls named Wisdom. Two boys were christened respectively Espen and Espn (pronounced Espen) after the TV sports channel ESPN. Five boys were given the name Morpheus after the huge success of the film *The Matrix*, whose hero bears that name, while the female lead in that film, Trinity, has now had her name copied thousands of times. Of all the girls' names released in the 2000 stats, though, we thought Rayon and Dung took some beating. And spare a thought too for those little boys called Denim, Coal, Doc, Legend, Casanova and Tuff.

And according to a recent report from Papua New Guinea, Western celebs are starting to have an influence on children's names. But at least people are being creative: names noted have included Elton Travolta.

ART

We know there's a distinction between genuine abstract art and your four-year-old's painting of

crap art

A sculpture made of manure was erected in Bulgaria's capital, Sofia. The sculpture is not only a work of art, say its creators, but a place for people to sit and meditate; twelve people can fit inside the sculpture, called 'Dwelling, or Something About the Gene', and the Mayor of Sofia was one of the first to take the opportunity to sit surrounded by dung.

mummy and daddy, but some art projects did make us wonder.

Damien Hirst is most famous for his artworks consisting of animals sliced in two and preserved in formaldehyde. A recent work was a table covered in cigarette butts, beer bottles, cola tins, coffee cups and sweet wrappers. Valued at around £5,000, the work had been created especially for an exhibition launch party, and after the party at the Eyestorm Gallery in London, cleaner Emmanual Asare swept the whole lot into his black bin liner. Gallery bosses were said to be angry, but fortunately were able to retrieve the components of the work from the bag and recreate it, using photographs of the work to get it right. The artist found the incident extremely amusing.

Mexican performance artist Israel Mora had an artwork on show at the prestigious Banff arts centre in Alberta, Canada for which he was paid over £500. The work was Mora's own semen, produced once a day for seven days and stored in a cooler containing seven glass vials. The view taken by detractors was that he had been paid to ejaculate seven times. But 'Level 7', as the piece was entitled, was defended by the Centre's communications director, who said that contemporary art can sometimes be very challenging.

Nordheim's Water Music or just a few crap tunes? A Norwegian composer, Arne Nordheim, composed a piece of music using noises recorded at a sewage treatment plant in Oslo. The city's 280,000 inhabitants generated noises in the plant every time they had a shower or flushed the toilet. Nordheim attached leads to a computer and aired the recorded sounds on thirty-two strategically placed loudspeakers below ground. Anyone wanting to hear the music had to visit the Bekkelaget plant because Mr Nordheim said it would be hard to publish the sounds since the ongoing nature of the work meant it would be constantly changing.

We know art sometimes has to be dangerous, but this is ridiculous! An exhibition about death and immortality at Groningen Museum in Holland was planning to exhibit a nuclear reactor. Dutch defence officials opposed the plans, however, fearing that putting the reactor, containing uranium, in a public space would make it a terrorist target. A museum spokeswoman said: 'We don't exhibit anything that can be a danger to our visitors. We have taken severe security measures to exclude real danger and I think the quantity of uranium is much too low to start a nuclear fusion.'

Two actors took performance art to its legal limits while acting an erotic play about Christ outside a cathedral in Santiago, Chile. Police objected to a scene in which Maria Barrios seduced Luis Guzman while he was playing the role of Krishto, a punk Christ, carrying the cross. She wore a transparent dress and groped her partner, who then dropped his trousers and revealed his penis to the crowd. Guzman, twenty-six, and Barrios, twenty-one, were charged with public indecency offences. Guzman later said that dropping his trousers had been improvised and wasn't in the script.

SORRY ABOUT THE DELAY

A man in Northampton received a Christmas card nine weeks late from a friend who lives just half a mile away. The reason for the delay was that Royal Mail had sent the card on a 10,000-mile round trip to Beijing in China, from where it had made its way back to Northampton. Nick Richards looked at the postmark and thought it said 'Billing', (a nearby town) before realising it was Beijing. Royal Mail apologised, saying the card shouldn't have been diverted out of the country.

Back in 1901, a council official in Reggello, central Italy, posted a letter to one Luigi Beccatini, asking him to produce a portrait of the king. Luigi lived in Leccio, a mere 6 miles away, but the confused Italian postal service sent it to Lecce, in the south of Italy. The letter rebounded between the two towns for many, many years before coming to rest in an antiques shop, where, by a weird coincidence, it was discovered unopened by one of Beccatini's nephews.

A man put his name down for a civil service job in West Bengal in 1968, and received a letter asking him to present himself for an interview thirty-four years later. Now running a snack shop in Calcutta, he was amazed to get the letter last week. At the age of fifty-two, the grandfather and father of three is far too old for a government job. Labour Minister Mohammed Anum explained that it often 'took a long time for a person to be called for interview'.

DUMPING WITH WEIRD ABANDON
The things that people throw away!

A walker out in the woods in Cook County forest, near Chicago, USA, found a suspicious barrel. The 55-gallon barrel had hazardous materials warnings on the outside, so the passer-by called the fire service to deal with it. They sent out their hazardous materials team who established that there were 55 gallons of white liquid in the barrel, but what it was, they couldn't tell. After careful inspection of the barrel they noticed a phone number and rang it, to find that the barrel was from a firm in Iowa, Swine Genetics, that supplied pig semen. But they had no reports of missing semen shipments, nor had police had any complaints about stolen barrels of pig semen. How it got there in the forest – and why – was a total and utter mystery. And just to add further intrigue to the story, the police, who 'properly disposed of the semen' were of the opinion that it was goat semen. The barrels are re-usable, after all.

Bummer, dude! Smugglers abandoned 26,000 cigarettes at Manchester airport, taped into the shape of two surfboards and stashed inside surfboard carrying bags. The luggage had arrived on a flight from the Canary Islands, and officers counted 1,290 packets of cigarettes, worth about £5,500, concealed in the most ingenious way anyone there had ever seen. So why did the smugglers abandon them? No one knows.

Judy Wiltshire was walking her dog in Basildon, Essex, when she stumbled across a coffin. She called the police who arrived and opened the coffin – she had been too scared to do that – to find that it was empty. Ms Wiltshire was informed that if no one claimed the coffin within a month she could keep it.

Twice in two weeks the ring road that takes traffic round the Swedish city of Gothenburg had to be closed. Both times it was turned into a complete hazard because thousands of golf balls were released into a tunnel. Police had no idea who dumped them there or why.

Not True, Unfortunately

In the course of a year spent collecting the weird, wild and wonderful stories, some are bound to turn out to be falsified in some way. In some cases the reporting was honest, but the story was a lie or a hoax. In others the story itself was not verified before going out on to the world's press wires, or was even cold-bloodedly invented. And, of course, some news organs may put out a story that is in fact an urban myth, either in good faith or simply because they were short of interesting stories that day. When we double-check our sources, these anomalies do turn up, but that's OK – that in itself is a part of the world of weird news. Here's one that turned out to be an urban legend, although it did pop up in a few news stories:

Steve Huey had some pretty bad luck before he had his incredible, amazing piece of good luck: he found he was suffering from an inoperable and fatal brain tumour. Doctors gave him two months to live, so Huey decided to end it sooner rather than later. He wrote out his suicide note, put a gun to his head and pulled the trigger. Later, friends found him on the floor in a pool of blood. They called an ambulance and had him taken to hospital where, within hours, Huey was up and walking around. Against odds of 254,000,000 to one, according to one doctor, the bullet had not only missed all the vital parts of the brain but had cleanly shot out the tumour. A movie and sitcom based on the story are now in the works, and Huey is writing a book and planning a national signing tour. Doctors were urging other terminal patients not to try what Huey did.

The fact that this was supposed to have happened in a town called Last Chance, Texas, is a giveaway. It also started appearing in early April, which makes one think that it could well have been dreamed up for April 1st. If it hadn't already been around for a while, that is.

A story that received a lot of coverage for its human interest angle was that of Italian woman Flavia D'Angelo, who, it was reported, had become pregnant twice at the same time: while six months pregnant, she had conceived again, and was carrying triplets. Eventually she admitted shamefacedly that she'd faked the entire story. She fooled many medical experts, who said her condition was extremely rare but not impossible. The truth came out during a court hearing called to establish why she hadn't registered the birth of her first child. The supposed birth of her daughter 'Denise' in December was never officially recorded, and the regional magistrate needed to know why. It now transpires that while many doctors were quick to offer explanations as to how the almost unprecedented double pregnancy may have happened, none actually asked for evidence or examined her. Ms D'Angelo said she was under family pressure to become pregnant and so she made the story up, and it all then got out of control. What a tangled web we weave, when we practise to deceive ...

Here's a story that pops up every now and then, usually with one or two variations, a sure sign that it is an urban myth. This is the version that surfaced this year: Stephan, a bunged-up elephant in a German zoo bit the hand that fed him, as it were, causing efforts to cure its constipation to end in tragedy. Keeper Friedrich Riesfeldt gave his constipated elephant twenty-two doses of animal laxative as well as liberal amounts of prunes and figs, then later returned to the elephant's rear to administer an olive oil enema. This coincided with a moment of massive relief for Stephan, who opened his bowels and defecated so forcefully that it knocked Friedrich over. As he lay prone, the elephant continued to empty his bowels, burying his keeper in 200 pounds of shit. Friedrich suffocated to death.

A Swedish woman found part of a severed finger in a bowl of prawns and was so repulsed by what she saw that she was violently sick. The finger had turned up in a kilogram bag of frozen prawns produced by Royal Greenland, who promised to give the matter their prompt and full attention. However, this turned out to be unnecessary because when the police took it to a pathology lab at Kristianstad hospital, it was swiftly and easily identified as a sea anemone. The fact that there was no bone was a bit of a giveaway, but nineteen-year-old Caroline Bengtsson had jumped to the conclusion that it was a finger without checking.